MICHAEL COLLINS

LEON Ó BROIN

GILL AND MACMILLAN

First published 1980 by
Gill and Macmillan Ltd
15/17 Eden Quay
Dublin 1
with associated companies in
London, New York, Delhi, Hong Kong,
Johannesburg, Lagos, Melbourne,
Singapore, Tokyo

0 7171 0968 2 (paperback)
0 7171 1076 1 (hardback)

available in this series:
Michael Collins (Leon O'Broin)
Sean O'Casey (Hugh Hunt)
C. S. Parnell (Paul Bew)
James Craig (Patrick Buckland)
James Joyce (Peter Costello)
Eamon de Valera (T. Ryle Dwyer)

in preparation:
George Bernard Shaw (Kenneth Richards)
W. T. Cosgrave (Maurice Manning)
Daniel O'Connell (Kevin B. Nowlan)
Theobald Wolfe Tone (Henry Boylan)
Edward Carson (A. T. Q. Stewart)
Sean Lemass (Brian Farrell)
Arthur Griffith (Calton Younger)

Origination by Healyset, Dublin
Printed in Great Britain by
Redwood Burn Ltd.
Trowbridge & Esher.

Contents

Acknowledgments

I acknowledge with profound gratitude the help, of various kinds, which I received while writing this book from Dan Bryan, Vincent Byrne, Doreen Callan, Liam M. Collins, Michael Collins, M. J. Costello, Colm Croker, the late Emmet Dalton, Nevin Griffith, Geoffrey Hand, Máire (Tobin) Hand, G. P. S. Hogan, Val Iremonger, John (Jock) McGallogly, Mairéad (McCullough) Meenan, Risteárd Mulcahy, Kathleen (MacKenna) Napoli, Dave Neligan, Eoin P. Ó Caoimh, Robert T. Reilly, Joseph A. Sweeney, Pádraig Thornton, and Alan Wolstencroft. My wife, Cáit, as always, was a great standby. May God reward them all.

Leon Ó Broin
Dublin
December 1979

1

The Road to Insurrection

1

On the main road to Skibbereen out of Clonakilty, Co. Cork, there is a sign pointing to Woodfield, near Sam's Cross, where the subject of this little book was born on 16 October 1890. He was the last of eight children, and his father was seventy-five years old when he arrived. Given his father's name, Michael, the child grew quickly to be a sturdy, handsome, intelligent, independent-minded, quick-tempered lad who shared the work of the farm and excelled at whatever games were played in the neighbourhood. There was football, of course, of the Gaelic variety, and hurling; and Michael liked to play the high-spirited Cork version of bowls along the country roads, defying the police, and to wrestle whenever he could find someone to take him on. Physical contact and the overthrow of a strong opponent appealed to him. His education began in the home, where there were always plenty of books around, as well as unlimited conversation about national and local topics; and before he was five he began to journey the two miles to the National School at Lisavaird where his eldest sister, Margaret, taught. From there he graduated to the school at Clonakilty which was farther afield. In Clonakilty he stayed with Margaret, whose husband produced a local newspaper, returning to Woodfield at weekends.

If it had been left to himself, Michael, as his schooling finished, might have preferred to stay at home or to do something more venturesome than join the very junior ranks of the British Civil Service. But there was no future for him at Woodfield, which older brothers and sisters had already left and whose eighty-acre farm was only barely sufficient to support his eldest brother Johnnie's growing family. So the experienced National Teacher at Clonakilty was relied upon to steer him through the Post Office entrance examination for boy clerks, and this he successfully did in 1906. Michael was then posted – and surely not by accident – to the West Kensington branch of the Savings Bank where his sister Johanna, or Hannie, was already employed. This was a fortunate arrangement for a boy of sixteen, for Hannie had a flat in the vicinity of the office and was able to take Michael to live with her, which he did for the whole nine years he was destined to spend in London. By March 1907 both their parents were dead, and Hannie necessarily became Michael's big sister and mother. She was a highly sensitive and deeply religious woman with an abiding interest in literature which she shared with Michael. She encouraged him to read and sometimes sat up late with him at night discussing books and their authors. He read Hardy, Meredith, Wells, Bennett, Conrad, Swinburne, Wilde, Yeats, Colum, Stephens and Shaw. He began to go to the theatre and was constantly to be found in the gallery in the great days of the Court and in the weeks when the Manchester Repertory Company came to the Coronet.

Hannie recognised, as Michael must have done, that a routine job in the Savings Bank was the beginning only of a career; so, stimulated by her, he prepared for something better by attending an evening course at King's College, but, for some reason that is not clear, he left the Post Office in 1910 and went to work in the city, first with a firm of stockbrokers and then with the London office of the Guaranty Trust Company of New York. There were other influences at work on him, however, besides his sister. He fell into spasmodic association with a hard-drinking, hard-living crowd from West Cork and got the reputation of being 'a bit of a wild lad'. But the wildness was superficial:he was merely going through the 'blast and bloody' stage of adolescence.[1] In the Savings Bank there were many Irish lads of his own age, and he joined some of these on the football and hurling fields, and also in the Gaelic League night classes, where love of the Irish language and of things Irish generally was propagated; it was there, we imagine, he learned to resent the mildewed jokes about Pat, pigs, shillelaghs and whiskey.[2] His parents had been native speakers of Irish, but they shared the common view that their children would fare better in the harsh world of reality without it. Ironically, then, Michael had to wait until he went to London to receive his first lessons in the language.

For Collins the Gaelic Athletic Association was a prime interest. He joined the GAA's Geraldine Club in London, was its secretary from 1909 till 1915, represented it on the County Board, and was the Board's treasurer for a period. The Geraldines were by no means a good club, and it was greatly to Collins's credit that he stuck to them for so long and was available to play for them whenever they could field a team. That was not by any means always the case, and a whole six months once passed without it being possible. Subscriptions were often in default, with the consequence that the club could not afford a regular place of assembly. Committee meetings were held 'on Wormwood Scrubs', 'on the field', or 'under a clump of trees'. A treasurer had to be fired for being undesirable and untrustworthy; and at one poorly attended half-yearly general meeting a discussion, long and rambling, took place about an item of three and sixpence outstanding on a dance. Collins regularly wrote minutes which he acknowledged were 'extremely pessimistic, not to say cynical'. How-

ever, things improved in time, and his last report
[4] showed that 'on the whole, the position of the club
was satisfactory'.[3] Collins himself must have been a
fairly good player: he was at any rate on the winning
side when England, represented by London, defeated
Scotland in the 1914 hurling final that was played at
Liverpool on the day the Great War broke out.[4]

Collins's London period – the decade from 1906
till 1916 – was one of profound political and social
change. The Liberals held sway from December 1905
till May 1915, and thereafter, until the Great War
ended, they led a series of coalition governments. It
was the period of the militant suffragettes, of national
health and old-age pensions, of political labour and
the rise of self-governing dominions, the period in
which by a Parliament Act the veto power of the
House of Lords was markedly reduced. It was the
period in which Liberalism threw up the conspicuous
figures of Asquith and Lloyd George, and when Ireland, with the movement of the Third Home Rule
Bill towards the statute book, was roused to great
heights of expectancy: at long last it looked as if
she was to have a measure of control over her own
affairs. Irish Nationalists, strongly organised and under
the leadership of John Redmond, held the balance of
power in parliament following the general election of
January 1910 and sustained the government in vital
divisions. In such circumstances the Liberals, who had
hitherto been comparatively apathetic about Home
Rule, took a new interest in it and embraced Redmond as the Irish counterpart of the Transvaal
leader Botha. He undoubtedly had many of the quali-
ties needed for the part.[5] With the exception of William
O'Brien and T. M. Healy, he led a united party;
his temper was generous and conciliatory and,
apart from the permanent Irish grievance about self-
government, he had a warm admiration for England

and Englishmen. He had a few, a very few, critics in nationalist Ireland, however — among them the adherents of Sinn Féin, those who read Arthur Griffith's propagandist writings or D. P. Moran's *Leader,* and, of course, the handful who belonged to the Irish Republican Brotherhood, the IRB.

Collins had met some of these critics in the GAA, in the Gaelic League and in a branch of Sinn Féin he joined in London. But, before leaving Ireland at all, his mind was turned away from the Redmondite policy of working for concessions through parliamentary action. He was an occasional reader of Griffith's newspaper, *Sinn Féin,* and he knew something of the history of the IRB. The theme and background of many of the stories he heard at home was of Fenians and Fenianism. One could not escape from them in West Cork, where in 1858 James Stephens, 'the Wandering Hawk', had established the first group outside Dublin of the secret Brotherhood, basing them on an already existing Phoenix Society, and sent them out to spread the gospel of revolt. The names of Stephens, O'Leary, Kickham and O'Donovan Rossa were as familiar to him as those of the neighbour's children with whom he used to play. Not surprisingly, therefore, when it was proposed to him in November 1909 that he should become a member of the IRB, he readily assented. It seemed to be a perfectly natural thing to do. And from the point of view of 'the Organisation', as the IRB was synonymously called, Collins was an ideal recruit.

The IRB constitution, which had remained virtually unaltered since 1873, provided that membership was to consist of Irishmen, irrespective of class and creed, who were willing to labour for the establishment of a free republican government. While preparing Ireland for the task of recovering her independence by force of arms they were to confine themselves to the cultivation of union and brotherly love among Irishmen, to the propagation of republican principles and the spreading of knowledge of Irish national rights. The decision of the Irish nation, as expressed by a majority of the Irish people, as to the fit hour for inaugurating a war against England was to be awaited — a provision intended to prevent a recurrence of impulsive outbreaks like that of 1867 — and, in the meantime, 'the Organisation' was to lend its support to every movement calculated to advance the cause of Irish independence. Members were to swear an oath solemnly undertaking to do their utmost to establish that independence, to bear true allegiance to the Supreme Council of the IRB, which was deemed to be the government of the Irish Republic, implicitly to obey the IRB constitution and to preserve the organisation's secrets.

This was the oath Collins swore at the Barnsbury Hall, Islington, on a November night in 1909. With the advantage of hindsight, it may be said that in doing so he was taking the most eventful step in his whole life. Everything of consequence he did subsequently in the political or military spheres turned on the taking of that oath. He was introduced into the Brotherhood by Sam Maguire, an older Post Office colleague, whom he playfully described as a 'bloody South of Ireland Protestant'. He was well aware of Ireland's acute religious differences and would greet Robert Lynd ('Y.Y.'), then writing for the *Daily News,* with 'And how is the Nonconformist conscience today?' He was himself a conventional Catholic, but, like many an 'advanced' man of that period, he was critical of the Church as an anglicising influence.

The IRB oath brought Collins into an organisation that had suffered many vicissitudes in the half-century of its existence. Numerically it had at times been so strong and its revolutionary ambition so evident as to be a real source of worry to the govern- ment, but by the end of the nineteenth century it had become an insignificant body and would hardly have survived without the encouragement and financial support it received from an American counterpart, the Clan na Gael. Three years after Collins joined the IRB there were only 1,660 members in Ireland and 367 in Great Britain; however, a revival was under way, inspired by Denis McCullough, Bulmer Hobson, Seán MacDermott and Tom Clarke. In 1904 McCullough, the son of an IRB man, had introduced Hobson, the begetter of many national societies, into 'the Organisation', and with him he embarked upon a reform, recruiting young men and forcing the retirement of members who had either become inactive or drank too much to be good either for themselves or for an ostensibly secret society. A Belfast man who was being squeezed out on this account offered 'a good man' in his place. The 'good man' was Seán MacDermott, 'a fresh, frightened young fellow whose mother had warned him against secret societies' and who 'could not speak for nuts'. McCullough saw him as 'the rawest bloody recruit you could imagine', but Hobson, recognising the promise of the man, raised a small fund, mostly subscribed by men who could afford no more than a few pence a week, and put him on the road as an organiser.[6] In that respect his success was undeniable. Deriving inspiration and encouragement directly from Tom Clarke, a Fenian prisoner who had returned to Ireland under a ticket-of-leave, and indirectly from John Devoy, the leader of the Clan na Gael, MacDermott became the prime organiser of the Easter Rising.

[8] The Ulster Unionist reaction to the probability of Home Rule became undeniable when in September 1911 an audience of 50,000 heard Sir Edward Carson declare that on the morning that Home Rule became a fact, they would take over the government of Protestant Ulster. In the following February Winston Churchill, then a member of Asquith's Liberal government, was prevented from holding a meeting in the Ulster Hall and was forced to make an ignominious exit from the city of Belfast. In September 1912 a campaign across the northern counties ended with hundreds of thousands of people affixing their signatures — a few written in blood — to a Solemn League and Covenant in which they undertook not to recognise the authority of a Home Rule parliament. Early in 1913 an Ulster Volunteer Force was created, thus making it likely that blood would be spilled if an attempt was made to force Home Rule upon the North. The situation grew more ominous when a 'mutiny' of officers at the Curragh revealed that in such an eventuality the Ulster Unionists could conceivably rely upon the support of the British army. A countervailing movement then developed in the South. Another Volunteer force — the Irish Volunteers — was created in November 1913 and proceeded to copy the Ulster Volunteers by importing arms from Germany under the very noses of the authorities.

The generality of nationalists regarded these Irish Volunteers as a means of defending the Home Rule terms Redmond had won from the Liberal government, but the IRB had more radical uses for them. The Brotherhood had played a major role in the establishment of the Volunteer organisation, had secured a majority on its controlling Provisional Committee, and had had Eoin Mac Néill, a co-founder of the Gaelic League and a moderate supporter of Redmond, elected as its chairman. These develop- ments were not at all to Redmond's liking, and he had no sympathy for the spirit that animated them. The Home Rule Bill expressly precluded the possibility of an Irish territorial force being formed, and, with civil war looming on the Ulster horizon, the very last thing he wanted to see was further drilling and arming taking place. Yet he could not possibly utter any public discouragement to nationally minded people in face of Carson's military preparations.[7] Within the next few months, however, he made a couple of moves which were to prove historically important. In June 1914 he assumed the leadership of the Irish Volunteers and appointed to the Provisional Committee an equal number of his own nominees including members of parliament, Justices of the Peace and priests. By the outbreak of the Great War in August, no agreement having been reached on Ulster's position in the political settlement, and it being essential to present a front of unity in the face of the German enemy, the Home Rule Bill was passed into law as it stood, along with a short measure postponing its operation for the duration of the war, after which parliament would have another look at the Ulster question. In September Redmond declared at Woodenbridge that the Irish Volunteers should join the British army. It would be a disgrace for ever, he said, if they remained at home simply to defend the shores of Ireland from an unlikely invasion, a role he had earlier assigned to them. This exhortation split the Volunteer movement in two: a Redmondite element comprising about 170,000, subsequently known as the National Volunteers, and a small minority of 11,000 who, rejecting Redmond's counsel, followed Mac Néill and retained the original title, the Irish Volunteers.

A company of Volunteers had been formed in London in August, and Collins from the outset was an active member. He had been promoted from the ranks of the IRB to being treasurer for London and the South of England, and when the split in the Volunteers occurred he was able to influence his company to follow Mac Néill, which was what the Supreme Council desired, though instinctively, we imagine, he would have taken that course anyhow. A result of the decision was that he and the London company immediately found themselves in hostile territory. They met and drilled in a gymnasium at King's Cross and were taunted, with some justification, for being pro-German as well as anti-British. Anti-British feeling was, of course, never far from the surface of Irish life and was particularly evident in some of the Irish societies. The GAA never admitted members of the Royal Irish Constabulary to its ranks, and Collins recorded in the minutes of the Geraldine Club the automatic expulsion of four GAA men for competing for England in the Olympic Games of 1908. As the war proceeded, Britain's enemies were accepted in some quarters as Ireland's natural friends. *Die Wacht am Rhein* and *Deutschland über Alles* were sung in public, and *Scissors and Paste,* a paper edited by Griffith, countered the currently exaggerated accounts of British victories with equally exaggerated accounts of German successes. In the United States the leaders of the Clan na Gael told the Germans that their friends in Ireland intended to avail of the opportunity to overthrow English rule and set up an independent government. Towards that end they needed German arms and German officers. An address, drafted by Sir Roger Casement, was sent to the Kaiser praying for Germany's triumph over Ireland's traditional enemy; and the Clan na Gael initiative, communicated to the IRB, set preparations for an insurrection in motion, including the appoint- ment of a military committee. In these preparations Eoin Mac Néill and the bulk of the Volunteers who followed his leadership had no part, nor any knowledge of them.

The recruiting campaign which Redmond supported, despite all kinds of rebuffs from the British army chiefs, continued to yield good results until the second half of 1915. It then began to flag, following the consternation spread by reports of the failure of the Suvla Bay landings in Gallipoli. This brought into the foreground the whole problem of manpower and the possibility of conscription, if raising the military age and pressure on government employees proved inadequate. Conscription seemed immediately impracticable to the politicians, but a fear that it might have to be resorted to spread among Irishmen working in Britain, and Collins began to give serious consideration to his personal position. The first idea that crossed his mind, and of which Hannie approved, was that he should emigrate to America. He consulted his brother, Patrick J., in Chicago, who told him that if he did decide to go, he would no doubt be able 'to land something there even if it came slow'. He would in any event 'be sure of a place to sleep and eat'. Business was improving in the States, pointing to a prosperous future, and Patrick had begun to make soundings for Michael among the banking community. He said that he would himself take a chance on emigrating, but that Michael would have to use his own discretion and do nothing that he might regret. He wondered how Michael thought the war was going, and he made no secret of his own view that the Germans would finish off the Russians – and then God help France and England.

[12] For whatever reason, Collins stayed on in London until the government introduced a bill in January 1916 making military service compulsory for unmarried men between the ages of eighteen and forty-one. Ireland was exempted, but the future of Irishmen living in Britain was hazardous. So he made for Dublin. His position in the IRB brought him into contact there with Tom Clarke and Seán MacDermott, from whose conversation he inferred that some manoeuvre quite out of the ordinary was being prepared in which he would be expected to play a part. While waiting for this to happen he divided his time between a job at thirty shillings a week with Craig Gardners, the accountants, visits to a Volunteer training camp at Larkfield Manor in Kimmage, and the Keating Branch of the Gaelic League, which was a regular hotbed of republicanism. He changed his digs a number of times, staying with, among others, Paddy Belton, whom he had known in the Geraldine Club. In the Keating Branch he made the acquaintance of three men whose close friendship he was to retain to the end of his days: these were Richard Mulcahy, Diarmuid O'Hegarty and Gearóid O'Sullivan. He also got to know Cathal Brugha, the branch president, but found him 'strange . . . not unfriendly, but oddly remote'.

The 'manoeuvre out of the ordinary' they were all waiting for was the Easter Rising. The decision to rise at Easter was taken at a meeting of the Supreme Council of the IRB in January 1916, during the presidency of Denis McCullough. Because he lived in Belfast, McCullough had accepted the office with reluctance, recognising that when action was called for it would be directed from Dublin, with responsibility falling on the Dublin-based members. This fitted in well with MacDermott's ideas. Through him particularly the IRB Executive had achieved a large measure of control over the Volunteers and had seen to it that as far as possible men of their choosing filled the important officerships. There were individuals like Eoin Mac Néill, however, who would have nothing to do with the IRB and who opposed on moral grounds the concept of a rising in the circumstances of the time, but whom MacDermott hoped would nevertheless turn out 'on the day'. A military committee was appointed 'of people who', McCullough said, 'could run the Rising. We hadn't the knowledge or the mentality.' But, though President of 'the Organisation', McCullough was apparently unaware that such a committee (usually known as the Military Council), consisting of Patrick Pearse, Joseph Plunkett and Eamonn Ceannt, had been in existence since May 1915, that Clarke and MacDermott had joined the committee later that year and approved a detailed military plan the others had worked out, and that Plunkett had been to Germany and had arranged that a cargo of guns and ammunition would be delivered in Ireland on a given date. Later, other members were added to the Military Council, notably James Connolly, the leader of a miniature Irish Citizen Army that had come into being in 1913 during the great industrial lockout of that year.

A series of quite extraordinary events almost ensured that the Rising would never take place. On the Monday of Holy Week 1916 the Irish government — effectively the Under-Secretary in Dublin Castle, a civil servant representing the Chief Secretary, who was a member of the British cabinet — received a warning of a contemplated landing of arms on the south-west coast and of an insurrection planned for the following Saturday, Easter Eve. That had been the date originally agreed with the Germans, but the Military Council had later decided to rise on Easter

Sunday, and a communication to that effect was sent to Berlin. The arms ship, the *Aud,* had already departed, however, and could not be reached by radio. Nor was it possible to contact the submarine which Sir Roger Casement had induced the Germans to put at his disposal. He had left them under the impression that he wanted to join the Rising, but his secret resolve was to prevent the Rising taking place. He did not trust the Germans, and he was totally confused about the situation at home. The *Aud* and the submarine U—19 therefore arrived prematurely; Casement was arrested when put ashore near Tralee, and the British navy rounded up the arms ship. They were taking it into Cork Harbour when it was scuttled, and the cargo sent to the bottom of the sea. A motor-car on its way to take over the British naval wireless station at Cahirciveen, with a view to establishing contact with the *Aud,* was accidently driven over a pier-head and its Volunteer occupants drowned. The part they were to play had been explained to them by Seán MacDermott and Collins, who by now was privy to the plans for the Rising.

The reports of these disasters no doubt gave great satisfaction to the government, since they appeared to confirm that the 'Sinn Féiners' (as they were incorrectly supposed to be) were no better at conducting a revolution than Emmet had been in 1803, the Young Irelanders in 1848, and the Fenians in 1867. A marked increase of tension had been noticed in the run-up to Easter. A general mobilisation and march of Irish Volunteers on Easter Sunday had been widely publicised. There were rumours of an intended attack on Dublin Castle, and a bogus military order was circulated to the effect that the government would raid named buildings in Dublin as a prelude to the disarming of the Volunteers. The happenings on the south-west coast had utterly changed the picture, however; and, as the authorities began to consider what they should do in face of treasonable conspiracy with the German enemy, they read in the *Sunday Independent* that Eoin Mac Néill, the President and Chief of Staff of the Irish Volunteers, had called off the mobilisation. He had heard that the IRB, with full knowledge of his disagreement with their ideas, had determined to stage a rising behind his back, utilising the advertised mobilisation and manoeuvres for that purpose. The news of the sinking of the *Aud* and of Casement's arrest convinced him that a deal, made secretly with the Germans, had gone awry, thereby ensuring that if a rising were attempted, it would end badly for all those embroiled in it.

But a rising did take place nevertheless, not on Easter Sunday but on Easter Monday (24 April), and under circumstances that we can only surmise. The seven members of the Military Council were men committed to action and to each other, men who by this time recognised that they had either to fight or be arrested, and that in the latter event the whole physical-force movement would fizzle out in futility. Some, if not all, of them had ideas about making a blood sacrifice. Instead, therefore, of waiting for the Castle to move, they resumed the initiative Mac Néill had taken from them and cloaked their decision to rise on a new date by first confirming his cancellation of the Easter Sunday manoeuvres. In deciding to go into action on the following day they deceived not only Mac Néill but the Castle officials, who were actually preparing a list of individuals to be arrested and interned on Easter Tuesday when one of the Castle gates was attacked by a section of the Irish Citizen Army. Simultaneously a number of prominent buildings were occupied. One of these, the General Post Office, in the very heart of the city, became the Dublin divisional headquarters of the insurgents, and

Collins, in a staff captain's uniform, marched there from Liberty Hall on Easter Monday in a mixed column of Volunteers and Citizen Army. They were led by James Connolly, the commandant-general of the division, with, on his right, Patrick Pearse, the so-called 'Commandant-General, Commanding-in-Chief, the Army of the Irish Republic, and President of the Provisional Government', and, on his left, Joseph Plunkett, whose *aide-de-camp* Collins was initially, and with whom he had spent the previous night in a city hotel.

Earlier on Easter Monday morning Collins had gone out to Kimmage to tell the Volunteers from Britain, encamped there since January, what they, whom Pearse had called 'Ireland's first standing army since the days of Patrick Sarsfield', were expected to do. He failed to impress some of them: they thought 'he was throwing his weight about a bit', while Collins, for his part, was not impressed by them in their various shades of ill-fitting green uniforms. However, they all went into the city on a commandeered tram, George Plunkett, their leader, insisting on paying the normal fares.[8] They disembarked at O'Connell Bridge and proceeded to Liberty Hall, where they joined Connolly's column and marched to the GPO, which they then proceeded to take over. Pearse stood to read a Proclamation of the Irish Republic to an uncomprehending group of passers-by while, from the building itself, stupefied holiday-makers, indignant old ladies, weeping girls and harassed civil servants emerged in great haste. A British army officer writing a telegram was seized and, to a laugh from Collins, dumped in a telephone box. A feverish rush ensued to fortify windows and barricade entrances. Shots were fired at an unsuspecting company of Lancers as they passed down Sackville Street. A boy of sixteen fell wounded on the pavement; a Volunteer fell beside him, shot by his own rifle.

For the next three days snipers and machine-gunners kept the insurgents on the defensive. On Thursday afternoon Pearse acknowledged that his headquarters had lost contact with the main outlying positions. The enemy had managed to secure a clear field for the play of artillery against the isolated GPO. The bombardment, far more intense than was antici-pated, lasted into the morning of Friday, when the leaders insisted that the members of the women's auxiliary corps (Cumann na mBan) should leave, going under white flags with the wounded to Jervis Street Hospital. The end was obviously approaching. At one o'clock in the afternoon a shell crashed on the roof. By three o'clock various parts of the building were on fire while the continuous sniping became more and more effective. Columns of flame and smoke increased with every minute. At eight o'clock the evacuation proper was begun. The insurgents moved out under concentrated fire into the area sur-rounding Parnell Street. There, realising that they were surrounded and outnumbered, they surrendered unconditionally on Saturday 29 April. The officers commanding the outlying city posts were likewise ordered to lay down their arms.

What precisely Collins was doing at any particular time during those few days it is impossible to say. We do know, however, that his first act on entering the GPO was to pour a quantity of porter down the drain and to take the names and addresses of all those serving under Plunkett's command.[9] Soon after the occupation of the building he was put in charge of the instrument room below the parapetted roof of the GPO, the part of the building on which the impact of the British artillery was most seriously felt. He experienced the flames, the heat and the seemingly unending shelling. Yet though confessing that, like others, he did the most witless things, he was never actually afraid; and he praised the gallantry of the men under his command, declaring that it reached unimaginable heights. One man who had reason to remember Collins from that week was Desmond FitzGerald. He had been given the thankless task of feeding the garrison, the Cumann na mBan women and some captured British soldiers, and was obdurate to all appeals to do better than he could possibly do in the circumstances. He was heard saying to one disgruntled Volunteer: 'Do you think that I am obliged to supply four-course dinners to you all, even if you are going to die for Ireland. Eat that crust and, as for drinks, drink water.' The only person who broke down FitzGerald's defence was Collins. Many years later FitzGerald recalled:

> Mick Collins, whom I knew by sight without knowing his name, and who had quickly shown himself as the most active and efficient officer in the place, strode in one morning with some of his men who were covered with dust and had been demolishing walls and building barricades, and announced that those men were to be fed if they took the last food in the place. I did not attempt to argue with him, and the men sat down openly rejoicing that I had been crushed. Apparently some of them had already been the victims of my rigid economy. But while they were eating, those of our most regular and assiduous customers who appeared at the door of the room were told to disappear quickly or they would be dealt with.[10]

Carrying crudely improvised white flags, the GPO garrison — less than two hundred haggard, weary, hungry and confused men, Collins among them — marched from Moore Street to the Parnell Monument at the head of Sackville Street and laid down such arms as they had retained. They were then removed to the Rotunda Hospital lawn hearby, where the 'bellicose and bullying' officer in charge, Captain Lee H. Wilson, picked out Tom Clarke, his brother-in-law Edward Daly and others and had them stripped and searched while they stood on the hospital steps. The indignity was long remembered. (In 1920 Collins discovered that Wilson was a district inspector of the RIC and had him executed at Gorey, Co. Wexford.)[11] On the following morning, thoroughly miserable, stiff and half-frozen, the prisoners were marched under a heavy military escort down Sackville Street, past the GPO — one can imagine how they stared at what was left of that building — and on to Richmond Barracks. 'The whole area looked as if it had been struck by an earthquake. Fires were still smouldering. Tramway standards were buckled over, trailing their wires about the street. The blackened ruins, the gaping holes in the roadway, the stench of burning — all gave rise to the sense of defeat and despondency which seemed to sweep over us.' This was what Liam Tobin, one of the prisoners, who was to become Collins's closest associate in later years, saw and felt. On the way through the city groups of people gathered to watch them, and among them were some who shouted and jeered. But whether they hooted or just looked on silently, they were probably of one mind with Redmond when, in the House of Commons, he spoke of the widespread feeling of detestation and horror the Rising had caused. The Irish nation had been let down and the scores of thousands of Irishmen serving in the war insulted.

The Nationalist newspapers were at one with the Unionist *Irish Times* in condemning 'a criminal adventure' supported by 'gallant allies' — a phrase taken from the Proclamation — whose only gift to

Ireland was the renegade Casement whom they had
.wanted to be rid of. The heroes of the week had been
the gallant soldiers of the British army who were
poured into Dublin, among them a couple of bat-
talions of famous Irish regiments. The surgeon's
knife had been put to the corruption in the body of
Ireland — a reference to the execution of the leaders
that was taking place during the fortnight following
the surrender — and its course should not be stayed
until the whole malignant growth had been removed.
The provincial papers likewise reflected public
opinion: the *Connacht Tribune,* for example, reported
a great public meeting, with a leading Nationalist in
the chair, which considered the action of ill-advised
persons in the county of Galway who, at a time when
the valour of Irish troops had done so much to shed
glory on the arms of the Empire, had chosen to shock
and outrage public opinion by bloodshed and civil
strife. The meeting expressed its determination to
follow Redmond and invited the citizens to enrol as
Special Constables so that they could be employed by
the authorities in whatever way was considered
useful. The National Volunteers (the Redmondite
section of the original Volunteer movement) were
already in some places engaged in the Home Defence
in order that regular soldiers might be released for
service overseas.

4

Their unpopularity was evident enough to the prisoners, but their primary concern naturally was to
discover what was going to happen to them. At first
they were afflicted by rumours that they would all
be shot, but then it became clear that the authorities,
with the help of the G (Detective) Division of the
Dublin Metropolitan Police and British Military
Intelligence, intended to segregate the signatories of

the Proclamation of the Republic and some others from the rank and file and deal with them by court martial. The result was a staggered series of executions in which Collins lost Plunkett, MacDermott and Connolly, three men for whom he had conceived a considerable respect. Connolly impressed him most. He had an air of earthy directness about him and he would have followed him through hell, he said, had that been necessary. He was devoted to Plunkett, had worked for his family, doing the accounts of Larkfield Manor, Kimmage, which was their property, and took meals with them in the course of which he talked literature with Joseph, who introduced him to G. K. Chesterton's *The Man Who Was Thursday*. Of MacDermott he was to say that, wherever he walked, there went with him the shades of all the great Irishmen of the past. Ireland would never see his like again. He, with Clarke, had built on the best foundations — by which, no doubt, Collins meant the IRB. To Pearse, Collins did not take at all: he was too vague and visionary and unrealistic.

Apart from those who faced the firing squad, there were many others who were sentenced to long or shorter terms of imprisonment. Collins himself seemed signalled out for special attention too. He was left in a batch of segregated prisoners at one end of the gymnasium in Richmond Barracks, until, thinking that he heard his name called from the other end, he walked down to where the bulk of the prisoners were congregated. Nobody told him to go back, so he stayed where he was until, later in the day, he was put aboard a boat at Dublin docks with 238 others and deposited the following day in the detention barracks at Stafford. It was 1 May 1916, and he was entered in the books as 'Collins, M., 16 Rathdown Road, North Circular Road, Dublin, Irish Prisoner 48F'.

For the next three weeks he and his fellows were kept in solitary confinement, seeing each other only briefly in the exercise yard. They were allowed to write and receive an occasional letter, and Michael complained to Hannie of 'the dreadful monotony, the heart-scalding eternal brooding on all sorts of things, thoughts of friends dead and living – especially those recently dead – but above all the horror of the way in which time refuses to pass'. Things then improved. The Irishmen were allowed to mix freely for most of the day as political prisoners, and Hannie came up from London, bringing a food parcel, of course, something to read, and the *Heath's Practical French Grammar* he had asked for. At the end of June they were moved to one of the internment camps in Frongoch, near Bala in North Wales. Collins arrived there well-dressed on the whole, but wearing no collar or tie, and his army boots were unpolished.[12] William O'Brien, the labour leader, was among the first to meet him, and for about three hours every day they discussed the past, present and future of the Volunteer movement. 'He struck me as being a good type and well informed,' O'Brien said. 'He told me that in the Post Office during Easter Week each of the seven men who signed the Proclamation was given a Volunteer attendant, and that he was Connolly's attendant.' He had spent a good deal of time on Easter Monday on the roof of the GPO with Connolly and was very impressed by his apparent ability.[13]

Collins's first reaction to the bleakness of Frongoch and the draftiness of a wooden hut was to get Hannie to send him a woollen vest and a pair of hobnailed boots. She could do nothing, however, much though she would have loved to, when he complained of being moved to a converted granary where it was difficult to breathe and where bedclothes absorbed the damp that blew in on the wind from the mountains. He made his presence felt among the prisoners, as he had done in Stafford, whether they liked him or not — and they did not all like him by any means. He was successful at sports and was beaten by only a few yards by the champion of Munster in a weight-throwing competition. He was tough; any show of toughness in the camp called forth an answering toughness on his part; and he gave any group he joined the feeling that something big and unusual had arrived among them. He was 'the Big Fellow'. It was not that he was just a bully, though his scowl, his fist-hammering on the table and his tornadoes of oaths and epithets gained him a reputation for being one. In after-years fellows he had met in prison recognised that there was a warm, soft side to him, and that his references to 'those bloody lousers' were reserved for his equals in the movement and not for subordinates. He was certainly rumbustious and terribly noisy, as Desmond Ryan observed in the yard in Frongoch. From a frenzied mass of swearing, struggling, perspiring players rolling and fighting over a ball — the description would fit a rugby maul better than the Gaelic occasion it probably was — he saw a wiry, dark-haired young man emerging, whose Cork accent dominated the battle for a moment. He then went under and rose again and whooped and swore with tremendous vibrations of his accent before disappearing again. 'That's Mick Collins,' Ryan was told, but the name meant nothing to him at the time.[14]

Collins had a great desire to improve himself intellectually. There were plenty of opportunities to do so in the camp. The prisoners organised their own classes in a wide variety of subjects, and what Collins learned in these he supplemented by private study. He was seen 'slaving away' at Irish between lectures; and his love of English literature flourished. Locked up in the evenings from half-past seven, there was an abundance of time for reading, and in the hut to which he was assigned there was a fire on winter nights and good company, among them some widely read men. 'Between us', he wrote, 'we haven't a bad library. A most weird collection though. To give you an idea — Service, Swinburne, Shaw, Kipling, Conrad, Chesterton, lots of Irish Broadsheet stuff, etc. etc.' Thomas Hardy was a personal favourite, particularly *Jude the Obscure,* and he asked Hannie to send him *Punch.*

All communications to and from Frongoch were censored, but Collins, displaying the ingenuity for which he was later renowned, managed to smuggle out letters to friends in which he frankly commented on the matter that was uppermost in all their minds, the failure of the Rising and the reason why.

> The actions of the leaders should not pass without comment [he wrote]. They have died nobly at the hands of the firing squads. So much I grant. But I do not think the Rising week was an appropriate time for the issue of memoranda couched in poetic phrases [he was thinking no doubt of the Proclamation of the Republic] nor of actions worked out in a similar fashion. Looking at it from the inside . . . it had the air of a Greek tragedy about it. . . . These are sharp reflections. On the whole I think the Rising was bungled terribly, costing many a good life. It seemed at first to be well organised, but afterwards became subjected to panic decisions and a great lack of very essential organisation and co-operation.

But nothing had happened, Collins appears to have reflected, that could not be put right next time — and that there would be a next time went without saying. Everything he knew about Irish history told him that. He differed from some of his comrades, however, in believing that the IRB should not go out of existence. He had a profound conviction that the example set by MacDermott in that organisation should be perpetuated. In that sense 'Frongoch turned out to be a veritable university of revolution.'[15]

In late December 1916 all untried prisoners were released unconditionally. Collins made straightaway for Cork and arrived at Woodfield on Christmas night to find the house in mourning: his grandmother had just died.

2

The Organiser of Resistance

1

He spent three weeks with his family and friends, 'drinking Clonakilty Wrastler on a Frongoch stomach' as he put it. Sensitive naturally to what was being said about the Rising, he was disappointed to find people 'too damn careful and cautious'. The young men were the limit, he said. The prosperity that the war had brought to farmers had ruined them, and they did not want to be caught up in the revival of Sinn Féinism that had been evident to Maxwell, the British military commander, before he left the country in November 1916. Most people were glad to see him go, none more than the Irish Parliamentary Party. John Dillon, the second in command, who did not share Redmond's recruiting zeal, protested in the House of Commons, in what the British considered was a disastrous speech, that the men Maxwell had executed were not murderers but insurgents who, however misguided, had fought a clean and brave fight.

By the end of 1916 the Sinn Féin leaders from being fools and mischief-makers, almost universally condemned, had been converted by the operations of martial law into martyrs for Ireland.[1] Before the executions, T. P. O'Connor said, ninety-nine per cent of Ireland was Redmondite; since then ninety-nine per cent had turned to Sinn Féin. These figures were exaggerated, but the trend they indicated, whatever about West Cork, was undeniable. A by-election in North Roscommon in February 1917 was won by the father of the executed Joseph Plunkett against Irish Party and Independent Nationalist candidates, the IRB playing a part in the victory alongside Sinn Féin, led by Arthur Griffith who had begun preparations for the re-publication of his paper *Nationality*. In May the Irish Party suffered another reverse in South Longford at the hands of Joe McGuinness who had been 'out' in the Rising and who was now 'inside' in Lewes jail. Both Plunkett and McGuinness acquiesced in not taking their seats at Westminster, thereby giving effect to a basic principle of Sinn Féin policy.

When Collins came up to Dublin, a city whose temper, Dillon warned Lloyd George, was *'ferocious'*,[2] future greatness was already writ large on him.[3] He obtained an appointment almost immediately as secretary of the amalgamated National Aid Association and Volunteers' Dependants' Fund, two organisations that, with subscriptions from the Irish public and the American Clan na Gael, provided relief for persons who had suffered as a result of the Rising. He had to canvass for the job, but was helped into it by a Provisional Governing Body of the IRB which had been formed in Dublin the previous August, under cover of the Gaelic League Oireachtas, and whose members included men like Diarmuid O'Hegarty who knew Collins's worth. The pay was £2 10s a week, and for this salary the organisation secured an employee whom Joe McGrath, who had filled the post temporarily, described as 'a ball of fire'. He seemed, William O'Brien thought, a typical Corkman, a pusher, and some people resented him. 'Who's this?' they would ask; but nobody could say much about him.[4] But he was incredibly methodical, never missed an appointment, and met genuine cases of hardship with immediate understanding. He lacked finesse and could be ungracious at times; but the work was done speedily and efficiently, and Collins made use of the opportunities it provided for other, long-term, IRB purposes.

With the release of the convicted prisoners in mid-June 1917 the IRB found it opportune to appoint a new Supreme Council and to proceed to the drafting of a new constitution. Thomas Ashe, who, with Richard Mulcahy, had led the Volunteers in North County Dublin in 1916, became President, and Collins a Council member. These two, with Diarmuid Lynch and Con Collins, drafted the new constitution and in the process deliberately omitted the earlier requirement, breached in the Rising, of a majority decision of the Irish people being necessary before a war against England could be inaugurated. Specific provision was made for a Military Council, which, it was emphasised, was at all times to be subordinate to the Supreme Council.

Ashe was not President for long. He was arrested for making a speech calculated to cause disaffection and died in Mountjoy Prison in September following a hunger-strike in which he was forcibly fed. The funeral was used to denote a revival of militancy. Three volleys were fired over the grave, the Last Post was sounded, and Collins, in Volunteer uniform, stepped forward to declare: 'That volley which we have just heard is the only speech which it is proper to make above the grave of an old Fenian.' In a shuffle to supply a successor to Ashe, Collins became Secretary of the Supreme Council and thus a member of the IRB's three-man standing Executive. In that capacity he directed members to see him before attending a Sinn Féin Ard-Fheis and Volunteer Convention that had been summoned to meet on successive days towards the end of October 1917. 'In one of the houses on the west side of Parnell Square', Robert Brennan recalled, speaking of the Sinn Féin assembly, 'I found a regular queue of men from all parts of the country. Mick, sitting at a table, handed me a typed list. It was the ticket the Wexford-men were to support for the National Executive.'[5] A trial of strength was expected between Eamon de Valera, whom the IRB were backing, and Griffith, whose programme was not considered advanced enough. In the upshot the anticipated struggle did not materialise. A compromise was reached involving the international recognition of the Irish Republic as an aim to be worked for, and Griffith, who had no personal ambition, stood down in order that de Valera might become the President. In the election of the executive, however, most of the persons on Collins's list were defeated.

Things went very differently at the Volunteer Convention. Of the four seats — apart from that of President — the IRB captured three, and one of these enabled Collins to become the Director of Organisation. The seat they did not gain — that of Chief of Staff — was filled by Cathal Brugha, who, with de Valera and others, had not resumed his membership of the IRB after the Rising and frowned on Collins's revitalising of it.

Notwithstanding by-election victories in South [29]
Armagh, Waterford and East Tyrone, the Irish Parliamentary Party, now led by John Dillon, continued
to decline, their place being taken by Sinn Féin, who
began the year 1918 with 1,250 clubs. The National
Volunteers, the military wing of the Irish Party, had
for all intents and purposes ceased to exist, though
a militant element under Colonel Maurice Moore —
it cannot numerically have been large — had reunited
with the Irish Volunteers. This had been achieved at
a meeting in which Collins participated, and was
followed by police raids on National Volunteer
premises throughout the country. Two further allied
events hastened the popular movement towards Sinn
Féin — the failure of the government-sponsored Irish
Convention from which it was hoped to secure agreed
Nationalist—Unionist terms for Home Rule, and
the announcement in April that conscription of
Irishmen for the forces was imminent. This had
become most urgent with the war running into its
fourth year. On hearing the government's intentions,
the Irish Parliamentary Party walked out of the
Commons and returned to Ireland, effectively throwing themselves into the arms of Sinn Féin. A national
anti-conscription campaign then ensued. A pledge was
taken to resist compulsory service by every possible
means, and the Volunteers acquired a certain respect-
ability, as well as a local leadership they never lost,
through the stand taken in association with them by
bishops and priests, parliamentarians and lay figures
who had formerly been hostile. Enthusiasm revived
among declining Volunteer companies, and recruits
flooded into them. The authorities were naturally
perturbed as evidence accumulated of Volunteer
parades and drilling and of explosives being seized.
They retaliated wherever they could, but men arrested

refused to recognise British courts and went on hunger-strike.

This was a policy the Volunteer executive were not too happy about, and they instructed some of the men under arrest to give bail and thereby secure their release. The first to do this was Collins, who was being held in Sligo jail for making a speech calculated to cause disaffection. He had been arrested outside his Dublin office in Bachelor's Walk and dragged to Brunswick Street police station followed by a friendly hooting crowd. He gave bail and went 'on the run'.

In April 1918, while Collins was still in Sligo jail, an extraordinary event occurred. A man, rescued from an island off the Galway coast, claimed he had escaped from a wreck. He was detained by the police, identified as Joseph Dowling, a former member of the brigade Casement had formed in Germany, was court-martialled and confined in the Tower of London on a life sentence of which he ultimately served six years. On the strength of this incident the government alleged that Sinn Féin was in communication with Germany in preparation for another rising, and on the night of 17—18 May they made wholesale arrests, including virtually every well-known leader of the time. The Germans had not in fact made any arrangement with Sinn Féin, but they had sent a message in code to the IRB which reached Collins. Written in invisible ink on a handkerchief, it expressed regret that the insurrection of 1916 had not been treated more seriously, and declared that the German government was anxious that another attempt should be made, in which event they would do anything they were asked to do in the matter of supplying military aid. It is not known whether any reply was sent; Collins's intention was to ignore the suggestion of another rising, which was entirely out of the question anyway, but to ask that machine-guns and ammunition be sent for use in a defensive anti-conscription situation.[6]

On the night of the 'German plot' arrests Collins attended meetings of both the Sinn Féin and Volunteer executives and warned the members of an impending series of police raids. He had heard of this from Tommy Gay, the librarian of the public library in Capel Street, to whom information of the preparations in Dublin Castle was conveyed by Joe Kavanagh of the G or Detective Division of the DMP. The warning was not generally acted upon; de Valera, Griffith and W. T. Cosgrave went home and were arrested and, with all the others rounded up, were deported to England and there interned. The only prominent Republicans to evade the net were Cathal Brugha and Collins himself. Collins, on the way to his lodgings, witnessed the police activity and tried to alert Seán McGarry, who was the Secretary of the Volunteers and President for the time being of the IRB, but the police got there before him. He decided to spend the night at McGarry's house: having been raided already, it was the safest roof to sleep under. In any event, his own 'digs' were a long distance away on Mountjoy Square, an area he had hitherto found convenient to Parnell Square, where so many national organisations had their places of meeting. He shared a room with Fionán Lynch (whose aunt was the landlady), Gearóid O'Sullivan and Diarmuid O'Hegarty; but it was already becoming dangerous to stay there, and he had begun to look for alternative accommodation. A house on the Richmond Road, Drumcondra, which backed on to the Tolka was at his disposal, and he did a great deal of his work there during the months following the 'German plot' scare. At times there were as many as eight armed 'itinerants' in the house. They had an improvised raft for crossing to

the grounds of a clerical college nearby; and Collins,
[32] always the practical joker, derived pleasure from
inducing friends to take a trip on the river and then
toppling them in.

3

In order to function efficiently as Director of Organisation (and, from March 1918 to mid-1919, as Adjutant-
General as well) Collins, practically on his own after
the mass arrests of May 1918, had to construct a
picture of the Volunteer movement for every part
of the country, the total number of men on the rolls,
the number that could be relied upon, and their arms,
ammunition and equipment. From that base he then
proceeded to make such improvements as appeared
necessary and practicable — regrouping, having officers
appointed instead of being elected which had been
the practice, and providing additional training. Regrouping was difficult. A proposal of his in November
1918 for dividing up the Clare Brigade, for example,
led to resignations from both the brigade and the
Volunteer executive. 'Now I believe Brennan [com-
mandant of the Clare Brigade] has the hell of a
grievance against me,' Collins told Austin Stack, 'but
that won't make me expire.'

His letters to Stack reveal the quite remarkable
steps he took to ensure that the personal needs of
imprisoned colleagues were attended to and that they
were kept informed of developments. Through friendly
warders he laid down a line of communication with
Stack during the time when Stack was at the head of
a group of prisoners in Dundalk jail. The result was
that the prisoners got the newspapers regularly and
could read of such events as the proclaiming of illegal
organisations by the government, the banning of
feiseanna, sports fixtures and public meetings, and

the public reaction. Stack could write to Dublin via Nancy O'Brien, Collins's cousin in the GPO; and from [33] Collins's letters, written every few days, he was given a fair idea of the variety of matters then occupying 'the Big Fellow's' attention. Sinn Féin, for example, was being laxly directed, and Collins mentioned specifically the danger of compromise involved in the Vice-President, Father Michael O'Flanagan, 'hob-nobbing' with James O'Connor, a Lord Justice of Appeal. He wrote of the production, under 'an awful lot of difficulties', of the first number of *An tÓglach,* a four-page Volunteer sheet which he was directing and distributing personally, and to which he contributed 'Notes on Organisation'. In one of these he told Volunteers to forget the company structure they were accustomed to see in the British army. Their objective was to bring into existence and train and equip as riflemen scouts a body of men capable of acting as a self-contained unit with such services as would ordinarily be required in the event of action. They would have to depend on the goodwill, mutual confidence and instinctive patriotism of the men for discipline and service. That principle was to govern the part-time Volunteer organisation as a whole. Volunteers would follow their ordinary occupations, drilling and receiving instruction at odd times. Battalion and brigade staffs would meet with difficulty; their 'headquarters' would be wherever their commanding officer happened to be: it might be a cottage, a farmhouse or the back room of a pub.

An tÓglach became the mouthpiece for the most violent antagonism to conscription.[7] One issue carried an article that called on the Volunteers to answer conscription, if imposed, with acts of 'ruthless warfare'. 'We must recognise', it said, 'that anyone, civilian or soldier, who assists directly or by connivance in this crime against us, merits no more con-

sideration than a wild beast, and should be killed
[34] without mercy or hesitation as opportunity offers.'
Collins liked the article, had many extra copies
printed off, and, through Stack, asked his fellow-
prisoner Ernest Blythe, who had written it, for more
of the same.

He sent copies of a booklet on infantry training
into the jail, and a long list of books of Irish interest
of his own. This included all twenty-two volumes in
prayerbook format of Duffy's *Library of Ireland*:
they ranged, he explained, through Tone, Myles
Byrne, Burke, Barrington, Mitchel, Mangan, Gavan
Duffy and Barry O'Brien, and there were 'lashings of
patriotic poetry'. Would Stack like any of these?
They were unlikely to be of any use to himself ever
again. Among titbits of political interest he mentioned that Harry Boland and Stack — both of them
leading IRB men — were the chief nominations for
the honorary secretaryships of Sinn Féin. Boland did
not wish ro run against a man in jail, but Collins
thought he should, and he sought Stack's opinion on
the matter. Other items of news included the fact
that Diarmuid O'Hegarty and some others had been
dismissed for refusing to take an oath demanded of
government employees. Finally, the Great War was
coming to an end, and the big question was how
Ireland would fare in the peace arrangements. Collins
declared that he was not optimistic: he believed that
they might have 'to go into the wilderness again and
be better prepared for the next clash'.

Ernie O'Malley, an up-and-coming Volunteer
officer, gives a picture of Collins at work in his capacity as Director of Organisation. He had been ordered
to report to Collins and found him in his office in
Bachelors Walk.

He was pacing up and down. We shook hands. He

jerked his head to a chair to indicate that I should sit; he took a chair which he tilted back against the wall. On shelves were green membership cards, heaps of *The Irish Volunteer Handbook*, and stacks of white copies of the organisation scheme. Behind his desk was a large map of Ireland marked with broad red streaks radiating from Dublin. He was tall, his shoulders were broad; his energy showed through rapid movement. A curving bunch of hair fell on his forehead; he tossed it back with a vigorous head twist. 'I'm sending you to Offaly,' he said. 'I want you to organise a brigade in the county. . . .' He had a strong, singing Cork accent; his brown eyes studied me fixedly. He pointed out companies on a map and mentioned officers' names. 'It looks like conscription,' he said. 'That'll make some slackers wake up.' He pointed out communication routes on the wall map. I was to improve and keep them tested by dispatch riders. He gave me a bundle of organisation schemes, instructions for the preparation of emergency rations, lists of equipment that could be made locally. 'Read that and see what you think of it.' He handed me notes on the destruction of railways, bridges and engines with and without explosives. It was signed by the Director of Engineering. He crossed to the window whilst I read. 'My bail is up,' he said. 'They're looking for me now.' 'They' meant the G men. . . . Collins laughed. 'Good luck,' he said, and shook hands.[8]

The Great War ended in November 1918 with celebrations in Dublin that the Volunteers set about interrupting: it was no time, in their view, for jubilation. Collins displayed a callous streak when he told Stack of 125 wounded soldiers who had been treated in the hospitals. 'Before morning three soldiers and an officer had ceased to need any attention and one died the following day. A policeman, too, was in a very precarious condition up to a few days ago when I ceased to take any further interest in him. He was unlikely to recover.' The government was alarmed at the renewal of Volunteer activity and the extraordinary vigour that was being put into recruiting, training and arming, and blamed the Irish Republican Brotherhood. It was reliably reported, the House of Commons was informed, that preparations were being made for fresh acts of violence of the most serious description, and a quantity of explosives, sufficient to blow up the whole of Belfast and Dublin, had been seized.

4

No sooner was the war over than Lloyd George called a general election which, in Ireland, resulted in the utter defeat of the Irish Parliamentary Party and the election of representatives of Sinn Féin to almost all the seats outside Ulster. The selection of candidates was conducted by an IRB trio, Collins, Boland and Diarmuid O'Hegarty — an illuminating example, it was said sarcastically, of democracy in practice.[9] Some men only knew that they had been selected when they received messages of congratulation in prison on their success at the polls. Collins became the member for South Cork, being returned unopposed.

On 6 January 1919 an attempt to arrest him was made at Dunmanway while he was speaking at a prohibited meeting. Police charged the crowd with batons, but Collins got away. He had, quite unknown to the authorities, been helping to reorganise the Cork Volunteers. The next day, back in Dublin, he was making arrangements for the summoning of Dáil Éireann, an Irish parliamentary assembly. That body held its first meeting in the Dublin Mansion House on 21 January. It met in public, largely as an act of defiance and for propagandist purposes; and, on the following day at a private meeting, Cathal Brugha was appointed President *pro tem.* of a ministry in which Collins was nominated Minister for Home Affairs. Collins was not present on either occasion, but in the preliminary backstage discussions he had opposed the plan to hold a meeting in the absence of so many of their colleagues in jail, and he had also objected to the introduction of a hurriedly drafted 'Democratic Programme'.

Among other absentees were Eamon de Valera, Seán Milroy, a veteran Sinn Féiner of the Arthur Griffith school, and Seán McGarry, whose presidency of the IRB entitled him — by IRB reckoning — to be regarded as the real President of the Irish Republic. All three were in Lincoln jail, and Collins and Boland had absented themselves from the first Dáil meetings in pursuance of a plan to get them out. A cake was passed in containing a rough-casted key which, when shaped with tools that had been smuggled in earlier, was to open a gate at the rear of the prison. Under cover of darkness, Collins and Boland were led without difficulty through barbed wire to this gate, but when Collins inserted his copy of the key it broke in his hand. By a stroke of good fortune, however, de Valera managed to push out the broken bit with his key and turned the lock. The whole party, rescued and rescuers alike, were then brought safely back to Dublin, Collins heavily relying on Neil Kerr, an IRB man he had known since 1908, who was increasingly active in moving arms and men in and out of Britain. A couple of months later Collins organised the escape from Mountjoy of Robert Barton, whose services were needed for a contemplated Dáil Department of Agriculture. A weight with a rope attached was thrown over the wall, enabling Barton to pull over [38] a rope ladder with which to scale the wall and jump into a blanket stretched out below. Another plan devised by Collins to 'spring' three prisoners from the same jail by the same method was so stupefyingly successful that half the Republican inmates escaped.

In the early part of April 1919 another public meeting of Dáil Éireann was held following private sessions at which de Valera was elected President of the ministry in place of Brugha and nominated a cabinet of five, as well as four extern ministers. Brugha was brought into the cabinet as Minister of Defence, and Collins relinquished the portfolio of Home Affairs in order to take up the duties of Minister of Finance. It was, he sensed, a historic week, 'the inception of something new'. The elected representatives of the people had turned their backs on the old order, he told his sister Lena, and 'we go from success fo success in our own guerrilla way'. He was hopeful that some good would result from the effort to have the voice of Ireland heard at the Paris Peace Conference. In May, at the last public meeting the Dáil would be able to hold for a couple of years, and which was convened for the purpose of welcoming an American Commission on Irish Independence, Collins in a lengthy speech described, as he saw it, the history of Anglo-Irish financial relations since the Act of Union, emphasising naturally the effects of over-taxation, the capital drain, the retardation of industrial development, and 'the price of enslavement that had been paid in emigration and poverty'. It was a subject to which he would have to give closer attention in the future.

Collins's work as Minister of Finance by no means consumed the whole of his abundant energy. He remained on the GHQ staff of the Volunteers, although in the first half of 1919 he ceded the posts of

Adjutant-General and Director of Organisation to Gearóid O'Sullivan and Diarmuid O'Hegarty respec- tively. In spite of this, his army responsibilities were increased rather than lessened, for his new role as Director of Intelligence became more and more important as unauthorised attacks on the police led to a state of war. In addition, Collins continued to be an active member of the IRB Executive, and at some time towards the middle of 1919 he became President of the Supreme Council, a post he held until his death. He thus guided the destinies of 'the Organisation' during the most crucial phase of its existence; moreover, at the time of his appointment the IRB constitution entitled its President to be regarded, in fact as well as by right, as the head of the government of the Irish Republic.

In June 1919 a three-day private session of the Dáil was held at which it was announced that de Valera had gone on a mission abroad and had nominated Griffith to be Deputy President of the Dáil in his absence. He had been smuggled out to America by Collins's so-called 'Q' Division; and taking up his call for the development of a constructive programme as a matter of urgency, Griffith outlined the case for a consular service, for action on land, agriculture, fisheries and forestry, for arbitration courts, for trade boards and for the establishment of a national civil service. The control of local bodies was essential to their policy, and the Dáil would aim to ensure their co-operation. For activity in these fields money was needed, and Collins, with the approval of the Dáil already given, prepared a prospectus for an issue of Republican bonds.

He was absent for part of the session 'as a result of enemy action': he had hidden himself away when he saw the police coming to arrest him, rejoining the meeting when they had gone. He was also absent from a brief session held in October. The Dáil, having been proscribed in the previous month, had gone underground, and Griffith had told certain members, including Collins, to keep away from its meetings. He was, however, present at the next meeting, in June 1920, and took the oath which, on a motion of Brugha approved by the Dáil in August 1919, it had been agreed would be taken by all Volunteers, Dáil deputies and officials, committing them to support and defend the Irish Republic and its government, Dáil Éireann, against all enemies, foreign and domestic.

Collins did not take this oath without some misgivings. He had already subscribed to the IRB oath, which was cast in similar terms, except that allegiance was promised to a Supreme Council which claimed to be the sole government of the Republic; furthermore, irrespective of his position as a cabinet minister, Collins as President of the IRB was under constraint to safeguard the interests of 'the Organisation'. There was a conflict here that had to be resolved, and Brugha no doubt hoped that this would be done by the IRB volunteering to disband. The IRB had no such intention, however; all they were prepared to do was to amend their constitution by declaring that, pending the establishment of a freely functioning republican government, they readily gave their allegiance to Dáil Éireann.

At this meeting in June 1920 Griffith announced that Collins as Minister of Finance had accomplished one of the most extraordinary feats in the country's history. He had sought £250,000 at home, to be raised in small sums, and this target had actually been surpassed despite the enemy's most determined opposition. The amount to be raised in the United States had been increased earlier from 1¼ to 5 million dollars, a measure of the great success of one item of de Valera's American programme. At this meeting of

the Dáil Collins obtained sanction for the establishment of six branches of an Agricultural Loan or Land
Bank, and an Income Tax Section which would
indemnify persons who paid their tax to the Republic
instead of to the British against losses caused by
distraint. He criticised a Commission of Inquiry into
the Resources and Industries of Ireland which the
Dáil had authorised and to which money had been
allocated. In his view it was only tinkering with the
problem, and, rather innocently perhaps, he boasted
that he would do in one year what the commission
had been given five to do.

When he became Minister of Finance Collins
acquired an office on an upper storey of 6 Harcourt
Street, the headquarters of Sinn Féin, and was there
when the building was raided by military and police
on 10 September 1919 immediately after the pro-
scription of Dáil Éireann. His first thought was how
to avoid arrest. He opened a window, hoping to find a
drainpipe he could climb down, but there was none
within reach. He then tried to bluff his way out of his
predicament. He gave a revolver to a typist to hide as
an inspector of the G Division entered, leaving a
policeman at the door. The inspector did not know
Collins — few of them did — nor did he suspect his
identity. Seeing him snatching up some documents,
he demanded that they should be given to him,
but Collins refused. 'What have they got to do with
you?' he said. 'And a nice job you've got, spying on
your countrymen.' The words seemed to have an
effect on the inspector. At any rate he allowed
Collins to brush past him and the man guarding the
door, and Collins, rushing upstairs to the caretaker's
apartments, climbed out through a skylight, reached
the building next door and stayed there until the raid
was over. He continued to make occasional use of the
Sinn Féin premises until Batt O'Connor, who was a

master builder, purchased No. 76, a house some distance up on the other side of Harcourt Street, and fitted a secret closet where, as under the floor of his own house in Donnybrook, gold pieces received for the Dáil Loan were safely hidden.

O'Connor also provided a skylight escape route. A light ladder was left in readiness which Collins could haul up after him; bolts were placed that could be fastened on the outside; there was an alarum bell; and the hotel boots next door was 'squared' to leave his skylight always unbolted. Everything seemed to have been thought of; but when the alarum sounded one day and Collins hurried along the roof he found that the hotel skylight overhung the well-hole of the stairway, so that to drop straight down meant certain death. He had to act quickly, however, for behind him was a figure in khaki. He let himself down through the skylight, then flung himself across the well-hole, landing safely but straining himself in the process. Nevertheless, he was able to walk through the hotel into the street and boarded a tram. Not surprisingly, after that experience he thought he had better move the Dáil Loan offices out of Harcourt Street altogether. For a while he used different places in Henry Street and Mary Street before settling down in St Andrew Street, where Batt O'Connor had prepared another hiding place for the gold collection.

3
Director of Intelligence

1

The year in which Dáil Éireann was established —
1919 — saw the beginning of the armed conflict now
commonly called the Anglo-Irish War or the War
of Independence. Indeed, on the very day of the
inaugural meeting two constables of the RIC were
set upon at Soloheadbeg in South Tipperary, shot
dead, and their arms, and the gelignite they were
escorting to a quarry, taken from them. The action
was carried out by local Volunteers entirely on their
own initiative. One of them, finding the official
policy of quiescence unbearable, had said: 'If this is
to continue to be the state of affairs, we'll have to
kill someone and make the bloody enemy organise
us.' The Volunteer GHQ's control of the movement
was manifestly tenuous, and reaction to the incident
varied considerably. Richard Mulcahy, who succeeded
Brugha as Chief of Staff in April 1919 on the latter's
appointment as Minister of Defence, deplored what
had happened: in his opinion 'It was an ill-judged
action with regrettable and unwarranted features.'
But Collins approved of it, and *An tÓglach,* which he
was in a position to direct, told the Volunteer body
that they could use all legitimate methods of warfare
against the soldiers and policemen of the English
usurper and slay them if it was necessary to do so to
overcome their resistance. De Valera, on the other
hand, spoke of subjecting the police forces to a policy
of social ostracism.

The British reacted by proclaiming South Tipperary
as a Special Military Area, enabling them to make
widespread raids and prevent fairs from being held.

Other signs of tension then began to multiply. Prisoners revolted in jails or went on hunger-strike. In England men were found in possession of explosives, and others escaped while being transferred from one prison to another. A military guard was attacked in Macroom and arms seized. Volunteers marched in uniform at the funeral of one of their officers, a member of the Dáil, who had died in prison. A Volunteer officer was rescued from the police at Knocklong and two policemen shot dead. Yet men jailed for the alleged 'German plot' were released, causing people to wonder whether the government had any policy at all other than to allow the drift towards the abyss to continue. Before the end of June, in response to the shooting of a Resident Magistrate in Ballina and of an RIC man during the rescue of a Volunteer from a hospital, further areas were proclaimed; a newspaper was suppressed and its plant dismantled. The country was full of troops, and armoured cars and tanks arrived in a steady stream. Alarmed at the prospects, the Catholic bishops put the blame for what was happening on a regime which, they said, was 'extremely provocative of disorder and chronic rebellion'.

In the second half of the year the war against the police intensified. It was very much more than a matter of social ostracism. Attacks on barracks, protection posts and patrols, in which casualties were inflicted and arms and ammunition captured, were the principal feature of Volunteer activity outside Dublin; the authorities retaliated with extensive searches, the proclamation of more and more military areas, and by putting provincial papers out of business. In Dublin a special 'Squad' of Volunteers, directed by Collins in his new role as Director of Intelligence, proceeded methodically to assassinate key members of the G Division of the DMP who were engaged in the detection of political crime. This was an element on which the government had tradi- tionally relied for suppressing national movements, and for that reason Collins paid it particular attention. On 30 July 1919 Detective-Sergeant Smith was shot dead at his home in Drumcondra; Detective-Constable Hoey shared the same fate in Townsend Street on 12 September; on 30 November Detective-Sergeant Barton was gunned down in College Street; and on 14 December a Detective-Officer Walsh barely escaped with his life in Drumcondra.

In undermining the British intelligence machine and enabling himself usually to be a step ahead of the enemy, Collins was able to rely on a group of four men within the G Division. These were Joe Kavanagh, the senior member of the group, who recruited James MacNamara, Ned Broy and Dave Neligan. They left messages for Collins at various places, often at the public library in Capel Street, or they met him at the librarian Tommy Gay's house in Clontarf. They would travel out separately by tram and, when Collins arrived on his old bicycle, as he usually did, they would have tea with him and talk business. Two of them were particularly well placed. MacNamara was a confidential clerk to the Assistant Commissioner. Broy was the confidential typist at the G Division headquarters in Brunswick Street and was able to make an extra copy for Collins of every report of political consequence that passed through his hands. One night he went so far as to lock up the sleeping constables in their quarters and to admit Collins, so that he might at his leisure read through the official files, one of them about himself. The first fruit of this enterprise was the issue of a warning to certain G men of the danger of being too officious. The home of one of them was raided; another was held up in the street, bound and gagged, and left as an example to his colleagues.

Neligan, the youngest of Collins's quartet of 'inside' men, had only joined the DMP in 1918 but had resigned on seeing the error of his ways. For doing this he got no sympathy from Collins, who directed him to rejoin and cultivate some leading Secret Service agents and intelligence officers who largely operated through 'touts'. The touts, like the officers, were Englishmen, and were at times brought together for consultation. Frank Thornton in his memoir describes amusingly how Neligan introduced some of these touts to Tom Cullen and himself in a fish-and-chip saloon in Marlborough Street. Assuming that Cullen and Thornton were English also, the touts expressed astonishment at the splendid 'brogue' they had acquired.

Collins's G men were a powerful adjunct to the full-time group that Collins as Director of Intelligence began to gather around him in July 1919. Theretofore the Intelligence Department, under its first Director, the solicitor Eamon Duggan, had functioned from Duggan's office in Dame Street with a staff of one man, Christy Carberry.[1] To do the job properly an expansion was inevitable, and Collins set about this by appointing Liam Tobin to be his Assistant Director and placing Tom Cullen and Frank Thornton in senior positions. Other individuals he introduced were Frank Saurin, Charlie Dalton, Charlie Byrne, Joe Guilfoyle and Joe Dolan. Collins saw that he had to plan the organisation of intelligence work on a country-wide basis, and this he did with extraordinary efficiency, advising commanding officers at every level about the selection and training of intelligence officers and how to go about recruiting agents. One thing he recommended was the employment, wherever possible, of individuals 'in a fairly high walk of life who openly boasted of their British connection'; and Thornton recalled what an amazing number of persons of this type who, on being approached on the matter, were prepared to work for Collins.

In government departments men and women were found with little difficulty to supply information; and through them lists were compiled of sympathetic and strategically placed clerks and typists. A lady on the staff of Colonel Hill-Dillon, the chief intelligence officer at Dublin district headquarters, proved particularly useful, and another lady working at British 6th Division headquarters ensured a steady flow of information to the 1st Cork Brigade of the Volunteers.[2] Contacts were made with army officers and men, and with members of the auxiliary police after they came into being in August 1920, a formidable number of them going on Collins's payroll. 'A Major Reynolds of F Company of the Auxiliaries worked for us', Thornton recollected. 'He supplied photos of the Murder Gang — F Company, Q Company and other companies of the Auxiliaries. Another Auxiliary, McCarthy, also worked for us. He passed over documents, and on a few occasions brought out files which we were able to copy.' McCarthy was dropped when suspected of a double-cross.[3]

Collins had 'friends' also in government offices in Britain, even in Scotland Yard. He ran an extensive correspondence with old IRB and IRA comrades, often adding to business letters a titbit that he knew would interest them. Thus, to Steve Lanigan in September 1919, speaking of the All-Ireland Final, he wrote: 'The Cork team gave a wonderful display of hurling on Sunday. In my opinion they are the finest combination that ever played in Croke Park. The Dublin team was simply not in the picture.' And outside government circles in Ireland his intelligence network, as we have already seen, extended to the police and prisons service. It also embraced workers in hotels and on the railways and cross-channel boats.

He was always apparently able to get information from the Post Office. Whatever his detective quartet missed was likely to be picked up in the central or local sorting offices or at the telephone and telegraph exchanges. Government, military and police mail was intercepted and selected telephone lines tapped. At an early stage copies of the RIC codes were obtained and 'broken'. Liam Tobin received copies of telegrams from the central telegraph office in the GPO. These were all in code and were addressed to district inspectors of the RIC throughout the country. Tobin possessed the key word and so had no difficulty in deciphering them. The key word was changed at least once a month, but, in notifying the change, the new key word was telegraphed in the existing code.[4]

The operations of this unique intelligence service were directed from an office that was situated a few hundred yards from Dublin Castle and that remained unknown save to a few people. The work of Dáil Éireann and of the Volunteer executive had, of course, to be done fugitively, clandestinely. The whereabouts of departments and offices could not be publicised, nor could they be concentrated as the interests of efficiency might demand. They were so small in any event that a couple of rooms here and there were sufficient to accommodate them. Such limitations were especially restrictive in the case of Volunteer headquarters. In fact there was no headquarters at all in the sense of a single building or suite of offices, and the staff rarely came together as a unit. Each member had his own office or place of work; the best Mulcahy, the Chief of Staff, could do was to form them under group leaders into threes according to their functions and to ensure broadly that each group knew what the others were doing.[5]

Mulcahy gave Collins his head, satisfied to know broadly what he was up to: their relations were always harmonious and frank. 'I opened and kept open for him all the doors and pathways he wanted to travel,' Mulcahy said, 'and we didn't exchange unnecessary information. . . . I had no occasion to be questioning him. Over many matters we exercised a constructive and practical Cistercian silence.'[6] The other members of the GHQ staff similarly facilitated Collins's movements and discreetly withdrew if by chance they found themselves impinging on some area in which he had begun to operate.

Collins's intelligence staff were located on the second floor above a small printer's shop, Fowler's, in Crow Street. They were supposed to be an 'Irish Products Company', but what they produced for Collins, who never came to the office, and for the Volunteers throughout the country, was information about the plans and movements of the enemy. (Later, when the work expanded, Thornton directed some of it from an office in the Antient Concert Rooms in Brunswick Street.)

To his intelligence staff Collins linked his 'Squad', led first by Mick McDonnell and, when his health collapsed, by Paddy Daly. Its members were available at all times of the day or night for dangerous or difficult jobs. Apart from McDonnell and Daly, the Squad consisted of Tom Kehoe, Bill Stapleton, Jimmy Conroy, Frank Bolster, Paddy Griffin, Ben Byrne, Johnny Dunne, Jimmy Slattery, Mick Kennedy, Eddie Byrne, Vinny Byrne, Mick Kelly and Pat McCrea; and through these men the process of neutralising British Intelligence was largely carried out. This was mainly a matter of shooting spies and informers. Two Squad men in turn would do this in the company of an intelligence officer whose task it was to indicate the target clearly and distinctly by a prearranged signal while the remainder of the Squad fanned out to cover the retreat.[7]

When forming the Squad with Dáil authority in September 1919, Collins emphasised its selective character. Its members were to take orders directly from himself and were not to discuss their movements or actions with Volunteer officers or anybody else. 'He gave us a short talk,' said one of them, 'the gist of which was that any of us who had read Irish history would know that no organisation in the past had an intelligence system through which spies and informers could be dealt with effectively. The position would be rectified by the Squad.'[8] They were paid a subsistence allowance of £4 10s a week, and sleeping quarters were provided for them in private houses. They were required to keep together in groups at these quarters at night so that they could readily be called upon: they were not to live at home. Their usual place of assembly was a house in Upper Abbey Street in the very centre of the city.[9]

Together the intelligence group and Squad constituted what Mulcahy called 'Collins's outfit', but between them there was a good deal of rivalry.[10] The 'outfit's' first spectacular move, in association with Volunteers from Tipperary who were 'on the run' after the Soloheadbeg and Knocklong incidents, was an attempt to assassinate the Lord Lieutenant, Field-Marshal Lord French. Some abortive ambushes had been prepared before contact was made on 19 December 1919. On that day French was to travel from Ashtown railway station to the Viceregal Lodge, and it was assumed that as usual his car would be preceded and followed by an armed guard. It was decided, therefore, that the first car would be allowed to pass, and a farmer's cart pushed out to block the passage of the second. But, as luck would have it, French journeyed that day in the first car, a policeman stationed on the road hindered the blocking of the second, and the third car, coming up at speed, opened fire, scattering the ambushing party and killing one of them. [51]

A vital link with all Collins's associates and activities was the slim, delicate and sensitive Joe O'Reilly, than whom few men ever got closer to 'the Big Fellow'. They had known each other in London, in the Rising, in Stafford and Frongoch, and, when in 1917 Collins came across Joe in Dublin out of a job and mooching about the streets, he saw to it that he was helped by the National Aid Association before taking him into his personal service. Frank O'Connor describes O'Reilly admirably as courier, clerk, messenger boy, nurse — and slave, for his devotion was boundless. When Collins was in the mood for relaxation, Joe sang the old ballads Collins loved; when he was out of sorts, rough and hard-swearing, Joe endured his bad humour. Like Collins, he went about on an old bike regardless of the weather, singing and joking on his way. His work was never ended. He maintained contact with Collins's multiple interests. These Collins kept in separate compartments as far as possible, but Joe knew them all. He could tell where Collins might be at any particular moment and what he was planning, but he also knew how to keep his mouth shut. And he was a teetotaller, which Collins knew was an important factor in his favour.

Collins made himself available for the transaction of passing business in various 'joints' in the Rutland (now Parnell) Square area. Two of these were public houses (Devlin's and Kirwan's) in Parnell Street, and the third was Vaughan's Hotel on the quiet side of the square. Piaras Béaslaí draws a picture of a typical night at Vaughan's Hotel with groups of men from different parts of the country waiting to see 'the Big Fellow':

The door is swung open, and Mick strides rapidly

into the room. He looks around, and all the men at the back rise and make a gesture to attract his attention. He scans them all rapidly, selects one, beckons to him, and calls him aside. In about three minutes he has got the gist of the man's business, made a decision, and scribbled a line on a sheet which he tears out of his notebook and places in his sock.

Then he calls the next man and quickly grasps his problem. He makes an appointment for that man at a certain spot at a certain hour next day — and woe betide that man if he comes a minute late!

With amazing speed he disposes of all the problems and sends the men away contented. So thoroughly does he enter into each matter that each man leaves with the impression that his worries are Collins's greatest concern. . . .

When he joins the regular frequenters of the place, his senior colleagues and aides, at table he does not at first sit down. His restless energy finds vent in various sudden movements which a chair would hamper.

His face continually changes its expression as he speaks or listens. He looks now grim, now jovial, now angrily impatient, now deadly serious, now impishly mischievous. When he encounters serious opposition he thrusts out his chin doggedly and turns his head round till it is nearly in line with his shoulder.

Frank Thornton arrives with a report of enemy activity, and Collins goes aside to discuss the matter with him, Tobin and Cullen, and quickly determines what is to be done. . . . Collins returns and announces he will stay in the hotel for the night. He asks to be called at seven in the morning. Gearóid O'Sullivan and Seán Ó Muirthile are also staying, and when he rises in the morning and finds

they are still asleep in bed, he enters their room to
waken them with a fire extinguisher![11]

Frank Thornton paints a similar picture of night life
in Devlin's from about the middle of 1920, by which
time Vaughan's had become unsafe.

Collins had offices throughout the city for what
might be termed regular purposes, and the location
of them changed under pressure. Thus at various
periods he was to be found in Harcourt Street, Henry
Street and Mary Street, or in Cullenswood Avenue,
Bachelor's Walk and Mespil Road, or in Dawson
Street, Harcourt Terrace and Brendan Road. 'The
Dump', Diarmuid O'Hegarty's Dáil secretariat, over
a shoe shop on the corner of O'Connell Street and
Middle Abbey Street, was an important clearing-
house and co-ordinating centre. Collins often made
use of Phil Sheerin's Coolevin Dairies in Amiens
Street, which was right under the Loopline Bridge.
In the private room at the back of the shop he would
meet men of the Great Northern Railway who
carried dispatches to and from Belfast or sailors
whose job it was to smuggle in parcels of firearms.
In Kirwan's pub he regularly met the warders from
Mountjoy, some of his RIC friends and other intelligence contacts.

Like Mulcahy, the Chief of Staff, who had twenty-
three hideouts, Collins had many places where he
could turn in occasionally for a night's sleep; yet, like
Mulcahy, he had reason to complain at times of the
difficulty of finding a suitable place. One safe and
comfortable house was Winstonville on the Malahide
Road; another was Furry Park, the home of the
Llewelyn Davieses which stood in a large expanse
of wooded land well back from the main roads in
Raheny. The name and office of the owner provided
a form of security of its own, for Crompton Llewelyn

Davies was the Solicitor-General of the British Post [54] Office, a recognised authority on taxation and land values. Collins found him helpful in understanding the British political scene, and his wife, Moya O'Connor, was a discreet worker for the cause. Collins, when first she met him, impressed her despite his endless smoking and big talk; and, as his work expanded and the security net tightened around him, she made Furry Park available to him for whatever purposes he thought fit.

Spies began to gather round. The first of them — better described perhaps as an informer — was W. W. Quinlisk, an ex-member of Casement's Irish Brigade. He introduced himself to the Castle authorities in November 1919, complaining in a letter that he had been treated scurvily by 'the scoundrel Michael Collins'. The letter, passed to the Dublin Metropolitan Police, was duly seen by Collins, and with it the detailed information Quinlisk had given to G Division on being interviewed. Ned Broy saw to that. Quinlisk was clearly playing for high stakes, for the substantial reward he expected to receive for delivering up Collins to the authorities. His plan was to make an appointment with Collins, who could then be easily apprehended by the waiting police. He accordingly made it known to persons who were in touch with Collins that he had important information which he could only divulge to Collins himself. A trap was laid for him. He was told that Collins was going to Cork and would be staying at a named hotel. The following morning a cipher message went out from the Castle to the RIC in the southern city giving these particulars. It was intercepted, the local Volunteers were alerted, and Quinlisk, on reaching Cork to 'interview' Collins, was himself interviewed by a group of men and deprived of his life on a lonely suburban road.

A Fergus Bryan Mulloy followed Quinlisk onto the scene and was given an introduction, in good faith, by a member of the Dáil. Ostensibly an army sergeant employed in the pay office of Dublin district headquarters, he was in fact an agent for Colonel Hill-Dillon, the district's chief intelligence officer. He actually got as far as meeting Collins in Batt O'Connor's house and suggested terms to him for supplying valuable information. Collins did not like the look of the man, however, and had him watched until evidence accumulated of his *mala fides*. He then had him shot dead by the Squad in broad daylight in a Dublin street.

Neither of these men, one would think, were top-quality agents, but the third arrival had some reason to be so regarded. He said his name was Jameson, but he was in reality the son of an RIC inspector named Burn. Small and plump, he came to Dublin wearing knee-breeches and boots laced up his calves. He put it about that he was an agent for musical instruments, and displayed a passion for birds, keeping three or four of them in cages in his hotel bedroom. More to the point, he carried an introduction from Art O'Brien, the much-esteemed secretary of the Irish Self-Determination League in Britain. Joe O'Reilly and Tom Cullen saw through him immediately ('he was nothing but a crooked English bastard'), but Collins, whose judgment of men could sometimes be at fault, thought otherwise, and introduced him to members of the GHQ staff, to whom he talked of agents in military barracks who would assist the Irish with arms and equipment. Mrs Batt O'Connor was the next to be alarmed when she saw Jameson and heard that he was to have lunch with Collins in her house. A date in January 1920 had actually been arranged, but Jameson tactfully withdrew across the water on some urgent business, allowing W. C. Forbes Redmond, the newly appointed Assistant Commissioner of Police, to move in with a raiding party which included his clerk — Collins's 'inside man' — James MacNamara. Fortunately for Collins, and very unfortunately for both Forbes Redmond and Jameson, MacNamara learned what was afoot just in time to be able to warn Collins not to keep his luncheon appointment. Forbes Redmond was then hotly pursued by the Squad and shot dead, though wearing a bullet-proof vest; and when Jameson returned to Ireland with a portmanteau full of revolvers, behaving as if nothing untoward had happened in the interval, he was tricked by Joe O'Reilly into believing that he was being taken to an interview with Collins, and shared Forbes Redmond's fate. He was basically an *agent provocateur* and, posing as a Bolshevik, had earlier worked his way into the counsels of the organisers of a British police strike.

Thoroughly alarmed, the authorities in Dublin Castle now offered a reward for evidence leading to convictions for the accumulated deaths of fourteen men. By any reckoning £10,000 was a substantial sum, but twice as much, it was believed, would be paid for the capture of Collins, who, formerly little known to the general public, was by this time well on the way to becoming a legendary character, a sort of Scarlet Pimpernel. The British forces became obsessed with him, shouting in every house they broke into: 'Where's Michael Collins? We know he sleeps here.'[12] And yet Collins was the most accessible of men; hundreds saw him every day, and he was fastidiously prompt in answering letters. One day a story reached his ears that Willie Beaumont, a former regular army officer who had retained his old associations, was boasting in Dublin that he was going to earn the official reward. His reaction was prompt and extraordinary. He got the man's brother, Seán Beaumont, who was active on the Irish side, to arrange for him to meet Collins, and Frank Thornton, who was present when the meeting took place, has [57] recorded how, at the end of a long discussion, Collins revealed himself as the man who, in the government's opinion, was worth £20,000. Willie Beaumont, completely won over, offered to work for Collins and was accordingly directed into the British Secret Service. From this it developed that Tom Cullen, Frank Thornton and Frank Saurin often went to Kidd's Buffet in Grafton Street with Beaumont and Neligan and were accepted there as touts by the British army and auxiliary intelligence officers who frequented the place. They became 'friendly' with prominent Secret Service men, among them individuals who figured later in the IRA list for assassination. Thornton describes one particularly awkward moment in their association with these enemy agents:

One day, one of them turned suddenly to Tom Cullen, and said: 'Surely you fellows know these men — Liam Tobin, Tom Cullen and Frank Thornton. These are Collins's three officers, and if you can get them we could locate Collins himself.' For the moment we felt we had walked into a trap, but it was a genuine query. They had no photograph of any of us, and a very poor description of either Collins or of us three.[13]

2

With Forbes Redmond's death in 1920 the DMP ceased to be an anti-insurgent force of any consequence; its practice had been to work on 'touch', on experience and intuition, so that when experienced G men were killed their knowledge died with them. Increasing Volunteer concentration on the RIC was showing every sign of reducing that body to a similar

condition. Violence on the part of the Volunteers
outside Dublin had hitherto been on a limited scale,
generally speaking, and varied considerably from one
area to another. The proscribing of the Dáil led to a
policy of aggression aimed at clearing the country of
the RIC altogether and enabling the public to feel
that the Dáil administration, despite the formal pro-
scription, was drawing increasingly closer to them.
A regular 'campaign of initiative' — the phrase is
Mulcahy's — beginning in January 1920 with the
modest intention of having a single barrack assailed
each fortnight in three battalion areas, so crescendoed
that many barracks throughout the country were
evacuated before they were attacked at all. Some
three hundred of these were burned down for propaganda purposes as well as to prevent reoccupation,
and the morale of the constabulary deteriorated
correspondingly.

In a review of the situation early in 1920 General
Sir Nevil Macready, who had been appointed to command the British army in Ireland, told the cabinet
that the RIC might collapse any minute and that the
DMP was absolutely useless. That was bad news for
Lloyd George, who had preferred to believe that the
conflict in Ireland, 'the Irish job' as he called it, was
a policeman's job, and that if it became 'a military
job only', it would fail. The conflict was never
defined, and the issue was obscured by attempts
to distinguish between war and insurrection, summed
up in Lloyd George's phrase, 'You don't declare war
against rebels.' He was unwilling ever to admit that a
rebellion existed which had to be countered by
military methods. Something had to be done, however, in the light of Macready's report, and what was
agreed on in principle, on the suggestion of the
Secretary of State for War, Winston Churchill, was
that a special force of 8,000 ex-soldiers should be

raised at once to reinforce the RIC.[14] But this was a decision that was to be regretted before the year was out. It had the effect of turning the RIC largely into a military body without military discipline – or, indeed, any effective discipline at all. The first contingent of these police reinforcements, the so-called 'Black and Tans', arrived in March, and the second, an officer element known as the Auxiliaries, came five months later. They immediately proceeded to make their presence unpleasantly felt. Their function was to provide a counter to terrorism, but Macready saw them from the very beginning as a pack of cutthroats who were as much an obstacle to the pacification of the country as the Volunteers were. The Chief of the Imperial General Staff, Field-Marshal Sir Henry Wilson, agreed: he declared that the government had embarked on a suicidal policy that would lead to the British being put out of Ireland.[15]

By the time these ex-soldiers started to arrive, local elections had broadly confirmed the results of the 1918 general election, and were followed by arrests, deportations and hunger-strikes. Endlessly through the whole of the year 1920 raids, shootings, ambushes and reprisals occurred in every shape and form, and scores of towns and villages were sacked or 'shot up'. British intelligence officers and some officials were shot in Dublin and Cork. One of these, a Resident Magistrate, had begun to inquire from the banks about the source of Collins's funds, a proceeding so threatening that it was thought necessary to eliminate him. The chairman of a railway company met a like fate, not on that account but because he was a member of a Viceregal Committee at whose importance we can only guess. His death drove behind the walls of the Castle a number of civil servants, including Sir John Anderson and Alfred W. Cope, who had come over from London to prop up the administra-

tion, and they only came out thereafter under mili-
[60] tary protection. Before leaving London, government
policy had been explained to them. The extremists
were to be eliminated, and, while that was being
done, constructive business was to be pursued with
representative moderate men. On no account were
they to tangle with 'the Arthur Griffith lot' if it
could be helped, but the Crown forces 'were to go
all out for Michael Collins or any of that kidney'.
Dublin, in a phrase of Sir Henry Wilson's that would
have amused Collins, was a place given up to spies
and murderers.

The Prime Minister was prepared to stand over a
campaign initiated by Major-General Tudor, the
newly appointed Police Adviser, for the elimination
of 'the murder gang', a fact that caused even died-
in-the-wool Tories to fear that they were drifting
through anarchy and humiliation to an Irish Republic.
But when Lord Robert Cecil said as much in the
House of Lords he was rejected. They had murder by
the throat, Lloyd George said. It was only a question
of putting down a small number of dangerous men.

A sensational case was that of the Lord Mayor of
Cork, a Volunteer officer, who was shot dead in his
home by masked Auxiliaries in March 1920: but
there were many other less publicised cases at which
officialdom connived. The RIC were given orders to
shoot suspicious-looking individuals. They might
make mistakes, they were told by Divisional Commissioner Smyth in circumstances that caused a
mutiny of the RIC at Listowel, but no one would get
into trouble on that account. Collins subsequently
had an interview with the mutineers. They were
disappointed in him. He was 'unimpressive': the way
he asked questions and took notes were more charac-
teristic of a civil servant than a military leader. But
within a few weeks Smyth was assassinated and

Collins had begun to direct to his own purposes the men who left the RIC 'on patriotic grounds'.[16]

November 1920 was an appalling month. On the morning of the 21st, 'Bloody Sunday' in the national folk memory, fifteen British officers were shot dead in their Dublin bedrooms, some of them in the presence of their wives. The operation was intended to dispose of Secret Service personnel only, but names were added by the Dublin Brigade to the list prepared by Collins's intelligence group, and these turned out to be ordinary officers of the regular army. This suggested that the functioning of Collins's intelligence system was far from faultless;[17] but the bulk of those put to death were members of a 'Cairo Gang', so-called because they were recruited in Cairo for a special task, and Collins excused the whole operation, cold-blooded though it was, by saying that he had to get his blow in first, otherwise he and his men would have 'been put on the spot'. The Cairo Gang had begun to drive Collins desperately hard, arresting Thornton, Tobin and Cullen on separate occasions but letting them go after rigorous interrogation.

The Gang had come into being, according to Thornton, as part of a British decision to set up a full-time Secret Service outside the army, working on continental lines with both central and minor head-quarters. Their location in Dublin was discovered before long, and the caretaker of one of the houses where they lodged was found to be the sister of an old Volunteer. It soon became possible to have an IRA man appointed hall porter in the house, and gradually to place others also in employment there. An individual report was then prepared on each of the officers and clearance obtained from a joint meeting of the Dáil cabinet and army council for their execution. During the operation three Volunteers were caught — one of them red-handed — but a Castle diarist wrote that none of them looked capable of the beastly murder of defenceless men in bed. The Irish were truly 'an amazing race'.[18]

On Sunday afternoon the inevitable reprisal occurred. Lorry loads of Black and Tans drove into Croke Park and fired into the crowd, killing fourteen people and wounding some sixty more. All this slaughter spilled over from a meeting in Vaughan's Hotel on the previous night which was hurriedly broken up by the porter, Christy Harte, when he spotted a raiding party making for the hotel. Collins, Tobin and O'Sullivan got away to a Gaelic League hall nearby, and, lying under a skylight with a table and chair substituting for a ladder, they stayed there until morning. Dick McKee and Peadar Clancy, the commandant and vice-commandant of the Dublin Brigade, were not so fortunate. Having been placed by Collins in charge of the operation against the Cairo Gang, they had left the hotel earlier, only to be arrested in their lodgings and put to death in the Castle on Sunday night. A sergeant in the British army, 'Shankers' Ryan, was later executed by the Squad for giving them away.

On the night of 22 November Jeremiah Mee, one of the Listowel RIC mutineers, was summoned to see Collins in an upstairs room in Higgins's pub in Upper Abbey Street. Important papers affecting the Irish Self-Determination League in Britain had been captured in Dublin, and it was urgently necessary to cancel certain arrangements for the League's convention. Mee had agreed to travel to London for this purpose, and Collins explained to him that he had been chosen because of his military appearance, as numerous soldiers would be crossing on the same boat. '"What happened to your little moustache?" was his very first question when we met,' Mee recalled, and he explained to Collins that the Countess Markievicz, the Dáil Minister of Labour, with whom he had been given a job, had insisted on his removing it because it gave him a military appearance. 'Be damned to her,' Collins said. 'She should know by now that a military appearance is the best disguise for our men at the present time.' He then gave Mee detailed instructions on how to prepare for the journey:

> Your most important requirements are a new pair of spats, a box of cigars, a walking-stick or cane and a good crease in your pants. Hire a taxi to the boat and get there just on time so that you will not be too long waiting before the boat sails. Get into friendly chat with some of the military officers. You can do this by passing round your cigars, and even if they do not smoke cigars it will at least be an introduction and will save you being questioned or searched.[19]

It was a stirring time. Fifteen incendiary fires were started in Liverpool, and a convoy of Auxiliaries was annihilated on 28 November 1920 near Kilmichael in West Cork by one of the Active Service Units that had been formed from within the ranks of the Volunteers. As a reprisal for this and another ambush in Co. Cork, part of Cork city was burned down on the night of 11–12 December. The ever-increasing number of arrests being made of persons believed to be connected with one branch or another of the national movement made it necessary to open internment camps in Ballykinlar, Co. Down, as well as at the Curragh and on Spike Island. By mid-July 1921, by British reckoning, there were 4,500 IRA men held in these camps, half of them officers from the rank of brigade commandant downwards.[20]

[64] Lloyd George professed to be displeased when Arthur Griffith, a man believed to be a moderate, was arrested in November 1920, but he did nothing to have him released. The arrest had two immediate effects in the Sinn Féin camp. It hastened de Valera's return from America — Collins setting in motion the procedure for smuggling him back across the Atlantic — and caused Griffith to appoint Collins to take his place as Deputy President of Dáil Éireann. Through his friendly warders Collins had little difficulty in maintaining contact with Griffith in Mountjoy, and the respect of these two men for each other was enhanced greatly as they jointly dealt with the first serious move towards a peace settlement. Lloyd George had authorised Archbishop Clune of Perth in Western Australia, who was about to visit Ireland, to lay proposals before Griffith for a truce leading to a conference. On 3 December Clune met Griffith and Eoin Mac Néill in the prison, and, carrying a promise that there would be no espionage, he saw Collins afterwards. He was surprised at the sweet reasonableness of men he had been led to believe were frightful ruffians, and he found Collins in particular most businesslike. It would be easy, he felt, to devise a truce formula with him, provided there was no question of surrendering arms. A formula was in fact devised, but when the Archbishop brought it back to London, Lloyd George confronted him with a bunch of papers which he said contained clear evidence that Sinn Féin was showing the white feather and was anxious for peace at any price. The *Daily Mail* carried a confirmatory story, and the Chief Secretary, who was a member of the cabinet, had advised that the measures being taken to suppress violence were being successful and that Sinn Féin everywhere was on the run. The papers consisted of a telegram from Father

Michael O'Flanagan, the Vice-President of Sinn Féin, another from the Galway County Council, and a letter from the Dáil deputy Roger Sweetman. Father O'Flanagan, responding to a statement that the Prime Minister was willing to make peace, had declared that Ireland also was willing, and asked what first step Lloyd George proposed. The County Council had passed a resolution deploring Volunteer activities and calling for peace, while Sweetman proposed a conference of public bodies.

Collins moved fast to dissipate the 'atmosphere of defeatism',[21] explaining to a rather bewildered public that Father O'Flanagan had acted without authority, and refuting a statement in the press that, in the event of negotiations materialising, Collins's own safety was to be assured:

No person in Ireland or anywhere else, had any authority to use my name. My personal safety does not count as a factor in the question of Ireland's rights. I thank no one for refraining from murdering me. At the present moment there is very grave danger that the country may be stampeded on false promises, and foolish ill-timed actions. We must stand up against that danger. My advice to the people is to 'Hold Fast'.

In another letter he dealt with a press suggestion that Griffith had been taken into custody in order that he might negotiate more freely and safely. 'Does anyone think', he asked, 'that Mr Griffith would be so foolish as to negotiate with anybody from behind prison bars, away from his followers and from his movement?' Griffith was not asking for a truce. If one was offered, it would not be rejected, but he had not asked for one. As for the Galway resolution, Collins pointed out that Cork, which had fought best, had suffered least, while Galway, which had fought least, had suffered most.

The upshot of all this was a declaration from Lloyd George on the night before areas of Cork city were burned down that 'extremists must first be broken up' and that arms would have to be surrendered. A safe-conduct would, however, be granted to some members of the Dáil to meet to discuss peace proposals, but there were certain members who did not fall into that category. Behind the scenes he was prepared to concede that the Government of Ireland Act, just passed, providing for two parliaments and a joint Council of Ireland was not the last word in determining the relations between the two islands. On the contrary, it was the first word, but Britain would never consent, while life and strength remained, to the destruction of the integrity of the Empire.

So the raids, hold-ups and arrests continued unabated, and on Christmas Eve Collins went literally within a hair's breadth of being captured in the Gresham Hotel. With Tobin, Cullen, O'Sullivan and Rory O'Connor he had gone there to celebrate. He had asked for a private room, but as none was available, the party had taken their meal in the public dining-room. They had just finished when a posse of Auxiliaries entered the hotel and asked to see who it was who had been looking for a private room. Then, going into the dining-room, they held up Collins and his friends and began to interrogate them. Collins tried to get away by pretending to be indignant, but he was stopped and searched and found to have an Ordnance Survey map in his possession on one corner of which he had scribbled '6 refills'. The officer insisted that this was '6 rifles' and in the ensuing argument forgot to ask what Collins was doing anyway with an Ordnance map. He took a photograph from his pocket and compared it with Collins's appearance — the British had never got hold of a really good likeness of him — ruffled his hair and then called off the questioning. After leaving the Gresham, Collins and company made a call to Vaughan's Hotel. They had hardly left there when the Auxiliaries arrived on one of the raids that made that particular 'joint' largely unusable.

Next day, Christmas Day, de Valera reached Dublin, and Sir Hamar Greenwood, the Chief Secretary, knowing that he was coming, directed that he was not to be apprehended without reference to London. In the estimation of the government de Valera was, like Griffith, a moderate, a 'political'. There appeared to be some justification for this opinion. Obviously affected by the length and severity of the war, de Valera suggested to the Dáil that the Volunteers were not strong enough to push an aggressive campaign to the point of decision, and that to ease the burden on the people 'a lightening-off' of attacks on the enemy might be necessary.

General Macready found Greenwood's instruction irksome. They could have picked de Valera up at a dinner party where they had reason to believe a policy of intensified outrage was discussed. By then de Valera had had sufficient time, he argued, to make up his mind about his future line. It was impossible for the army to carry out a repressive policy if it was forced to work with one hand tied behind its back.

And so the cruel year 1920 ended.

4

The Dáil had meanwhile been in a state of hibernation, almost of suspense. It had only met three times in the whole of 1920, and then in private, and the meeting called for the 21 January 1921, also a private meeting, had to be adjourned till the following day because of the absence of de Valera, Collins and [68] Brugha, who, it was feared, were in serious danger of being tracked down and captured. The general situation was obviously very bad; a deputy inquired if the Volunteers were being cowed, and what chance there was of holding out for another year. That was a question that might have astonished Brugha, who in November had spoken optimistically about the military position, though his statement had seemed absurd to GHQ.

The Dáil meeting, at which the President made his statement questioning the value of aggressive tactics, concentrated largely on Deputy Roger Sweetman's public criticisms. He believed that the Soloheadbeg incident and the 'Bloody Sunday' shootings were murders and he explained that the purpose of the conferences of public bodies which he had proposed was not to enable negotiations with the British to take place but to prepare the way for a preliminary truce. However, he got no support from deputies and felt obliged to resign his Dáil seat. Collins, in the course of the discussion, spoke in criticism of 'the few irresponsible meddlers'. No deputy, he said, should step into the enemy's net at such a critical time. It would be better to give moral support to the Volunteers rather than find fault with men who were carrying on a fight against odds never before known. This was generally accepted to be the prelude to the assumption by the Dáil in March 1921 of full responsibility for the actions of the Volunteers, declaring them not to be the acts of irresponsible individuals or groups or, as the British would have it, of a murder gang. Another statement which the deputies took away with them from the meeting was also based on what Collins had earlier said publicly. It was the injunction to 'hold fast'. To that injunction de Valera had added that they were not to seek an immediate under single direction, whereas on the government side there was little evidence of co-operation between the civil authorities, the police and the military. The blind hitting of the Black and Tans and Auxiliaries had had an effective initial impact; but they were now getting as much as they gave, for the gunmen were killing them, while they as often as not raided, damaged and insulted inoffensive people and in the process hardened opinion in favour of the extremists and against the Crown. These were the views of Sir Warren Fisher, the Civil Service head of the Treasury, who had been over to Ireland to see for himself and had consulted, among others, the high-powered team of officials under Sir John Anderson he had installed in the Castle the previous year.

Fisher, we think, was in error in speaking of the single control of the exponents of physical force on the Sinn Féin side, but he was notably perceptive when he said that the gunmen were paying the 50,000 organised and disciplined soldiers of the regular army in Ireland the compliment of avoiding serious attacks on them. That appears generally to have been the case. Since 'Bloody Sunday' there had been an upsurge of activity by the British army.[1] In the martial law area (the whole of the province of Munster and the two South Leinster counties of Kilkenny and Wexford) they had been authorised to inflict indiscriminate punishments in retaliation to outrages. The first of these 'official reprisals' took place in Midleton, Co. Cork, on 1 January 1921, seven houses being destroyed after an ambush in which three RIC men were killed. The result was an outcry in the English press and retaliation by the Volunteers against Unionist property. The attacks on police barracks, patrols and individual constables were continued, but an extension of the campaign to disrupt communications was checked to some extent by compelling civilians to repair trenched roads and broken bridges. Inevitably Woodfield, the Collinses' house in West Cork, suffered. Two officers of the Essex Regiment, which had had many encounters with the Volunteers (now increasingly known as the Irish Republican Army or IRA), arrived one evening in April to announce that they had orders to burn the place. The children's bedclothes might be moved, but nothing else. Young men, taken as hostages, were made to pile hay inside the house and sprinkle it with petrol which the officers then set alight. And, rounding off the episode, Collins's brother Johnnie, on his way home from a County Council meeting, was arrested and interned on Spike Island.

The involvement of the military assumed dramatic proportions in Dublin. Large-scale area searches were begun in mid-January 1921, the first of them, wryly code-named Optimist, being ostensibly aimed at capturing Collins.[2] Over six hundred troops sealed off a part of the city centre and for two days searched it block by block. A similar operation was then conducted in the Mountjoy Square area; but in neither instance was any arrest of importance made. Again there was evidence of counter-action by the IRA resulting from the formation of a full-time, fifty-strong Active Service Unit within the Dublin Brigade. Troop-carrying lorries were subjected to frequent ambushes in the city streets, to discourage which the British army resorted to carrying hostages. The practice was abandoned when it was found that wire mesh could ward off a grenade equally effectively. One of the Active Service Unit's ambushes nearly brought about the capture of Collins. He had gone out to Gay's house in Clontarf, in a motor-car he occasionally used, to meet Broy, MacNamara and Neligan and was giving them a lift back to town when, at Newcomen Bridge, they ran into the aftermath of an attack on a military lorry and were ordered out of the car by soldiers. Collins sprang out at once, ready to run for it if necessary, but the others produced their police passes. 'These ambushes are a disgrace,' said Collins as the officer in charge described what had happened, but he did not delay to discuss the matter further. In response to Broy's 'Step in, Sergeant,' Collins joined the others in the car and they hurried away.

The resilience of the IRA, their ability to 'hold on' and even to carry the battle to the enemy, was spectacularly demonstrated in mid-March. In recent weeks they had suffered significantly. Apart from the twenty murder cases Greenwood had told the Prime Minister about, and which were prosecuted to conviction and to the scaffold or firing squad, the Cork IRA had been badly hit on a couple of occasions. An Active Service Unit at Clonmult in the east of the county was wiped out in February; and elsewhere six unarmed Volunteers were captured and subsequently killed, allegedly in a hand-to-hand struggle. The balance was largely restored when a flying column under Tom Barry achieved 'the most celebrated rebel success of the period' at Crossbarry in West Cork on 19 March. It did so by fighting its way out of an encircling military movement, dislocating a major search operation and inflicting heavy casualties. Macready called this engagement, which lasted about two hours, the nearest approach to actual warfare, as contrasted with ambushes, that had occurred.[3] Collins's delight was unbounded when news of it reached him. He had a high opinion of Barry, whom he had recently seen in Dublin, and Barry's regard for him shines through what he wrote of that visit:

The outstanding figure in all GHQ was Michael Collins, Director of Intelligence. This man was, without a shadow of doubt, the effective driving force and the backbone at GHQ of the armed action of the nation.... A tireless, ruthless, dominating man of great capacity, he worked like a trojan in innumerable capacities to defeat the enemy. [73]

Barry saw Collins arriving at Vaughan's Hotel one evening at 6.30, swallowing his tea, and then interviewing officers from five country units, advising, encouraging or reprimanding. To one officer from a particularly inefficient unit who asked for arms, Collins, with a scowl on his face, his hands deep in his pockets, his right foot pawing the ground, shot back: 'What the hell does a lot of lousers like you want arms for? You have rifles and revolvers galore, but you have never yet used them. A single bowsy Black and Tan is walking around your area alone for six months terrorising and shooting people and ye are afraid to tackle him. Get to hell out of this and don't come back until ye have done some fighting.' Collins took Barry all over the city to see what GHQ was doing and to meet de Valera and Brugha. One night while returning on an outside car they ran into a road-block manned by about fifty Auxiliaries. Collins had just enough time to whisper 'Act drunk' when they were taken off the car and searched. Collins put on such a first-class performance, joking and blasting in turn, that he quickly had the whole search-party in good humour. Barry was astounded at this display of nonchalance, but was none too pleased when Collins accused him of being 'a windy West Cork beggar'.[4]

Events like Crossbarry and the storming of the strongly fortified RIC barracks in Roscarbery a few days later may have been a factor in causing the Prime Minister to reconsider the position. The whole business of pacifying Ireland was being unduly prolonged, and he had become sceptical of Greenwood's progress reports. At any rate he was observed to be in a yielding mood towards the end of March[5] and prepared to concede Dominion Home Rule for twenty-six counties with reservations about defence and foreign policy. And in April, no doubt hoping to sweeten the atmosphere, he withdrew Lord French from Ireland and sent over in his place a Catholic Viceroy, Lord FitzAlan, who was known to be unhappy about a coercive policy[6] under cover of which in March, during curfew hours, in their own houses and in front of their wives, the Mayor of Limerick, the ex-Mayor and a serving Volunteer had been murdered.

While Collins continued to maintain regular communication with the commanding officer or intelligence officer of every live Volunteer brigade, it is evident from a scathing criticism from GHQ in March 1921 that the IRA in rural areas had, generally speaking, a very faulty grasp of the nature and techniques of intelligence work.[7] On the other hand, under Brigadier-General Ormonde Winter, British Intelligence, long defective, had improved significantly. The discovery of official papers in a raid on a Dublin flat led to the arrest of Broy early in 1921 and to his lodgment in Arbour Hill military prison, where Sinn Féin prisoners spat upon him, knowing nothing of his association with Collins. Collins immediately sent Kavanagh out of the country, both for the police officer's own protection and to strengthen Broy's defence by leaving Winter to think that it was Kavanagh rather than Broy who had been working for the enemy. About the same time MacNamara was dismissed from the force without any charge being preferred against him. Thus only Neligan was left of Collins's 'inside' group.

This undoubtedly had a detrimental effect on IRA

Intelligence generally. It deprived Collins of the warning system on which he had greatly relied, and made his personal position more perilous. His Finance Department in Mary Street was visited by the Auxiliaries one day while he was on the premises, but he avoided arrest by meeting the raiders on the stairs and allowing himself to be searched. Nothing being found on him — he rarely carried a gun — he was allowed to go. An intended raid on his office on Brendan Road was muffed, the officer in charge of the operation mislaying the precise address. The private house on Mespil Road where he did his intelligence work was visited by the Tans on 1 April, but the crucial records, deposited in a specially constructed hiding-place, were not discovered. Collins was absent at the time, and his lady secretary cleverly managed to warn him to stay away. Mulcahy, the Chief of Staff, was much less fortunate when a house in which he was staying was raided. He got out of bed and clambered along the rooftops to safety in his nightclothes, but left an attaché case full of papers behind him for Winter to study at his leisure.

A serious setback was the arrest of Seán Mac Eoin, 'the Blacksmith of Ballinalee', who had won wide renown as the commandant of the Longford Brigade and leader of a flying column. Collins greatly admired him. In March, with the net tightening every day, Mac Eoin came to Dublin in response to a call from Brugha, the Minister of Defence, who wanted him to lead a party to London to wipe out the entire British cabinet. He refused to listen to Mac Eoin's objections and insisted that he should be ready to travel within a few days. Mac Eoin went to Mulcahy who, busy with other matters, referred him to Collins. Collins fumed when he saw Mac Eoin. 'What the hell has you up here?' he shouted. 'You should be at home attending to your business.' Mac Eoin explained, and Collins

exploded. 'This is madness,' he cried. 'Do you think
[76] that England has the makings of only one cabinet?'
An earlier proposal along the same lines had been
rejected by Collins himself, and Mulcahy now
rejected the variant that had been put to Mac Eoin.
Brugha persisted, however, and actually took a group
personally to London, but to no avail.[8] The earlier
proposal that Collins turned down had involved a
study by Liam Tobin and two colleagues of the movements of cabinet ministers in London over an extended
period. Collins came over to discuss the possibilities
with Tobin and came to the conclusion that 'The
only way of getting the British cabinet collectively
would be in Downing Street, and that would certainly
mean writing off whoever did the job. . . . The project
was not really practicable.'[9]

Another project mooted — this time by Collins
himself — during this visit to London fits Béaslaí's
description of Collins as 'impishly mischievous'.
'Collins brought Tobin into Westminster Abbey
during a service. Tobin tried to behave correctly,
standing and sitting according to what was going on,
but Collins took out a paper and began to read it,
having to be reproved by a verger. At the end of the
service they began to follow a verger-led group
around, but Collins soon took Tobin aside to where
the Coronation Chair is. To Tobin's consternation
he suggested that Tobin should try, with the London
Volunteers, to smuggle it back to Ireland. Tobin did
discuss the matter with the London Volunteers, but
nothing came of it.' And anyway, when he returned
to Dublin he found that there was considerable doubt
as to whether the Coronation Stone is really the Lia
Fáil, the Irish Stone of Destiny.[10]

Mac Eoin's visit to Dublin ended badly. He was
recognised, and on his way back to Longford was
arrested. He managed to get away from his captors

in Mullingar, but was wounded and rearrested. Collins was grievously affected when he heard the news. Writing to the 2nd Cork Brigade, he said: 'You will have seen about our friend. It is simply disastrous. They seem to have sent a pack up to town to get him. Evidently they got information that he was here, and they appear to have drawn a cordon across the country against his return.' He then added a sentence that throws a revealing light on the military situation. *'Cork'*, he wrote, *'will be fighting alone now.'*

To appreciate the significance of that judgment it should be explained that, apart from Dublin and some secondary country areas like Longford, the Irish GHQ recognised a 'war zone' consisting of the counties of Kerry, Limerick, Tipperary and, above all, Cork.[11] Cork had been battling bravely, as we have seen, and Collins praised without stint the successes at Crossbarry and Roscarbery. But there were limits to what even Cork could do, and none was more restrictive than the shortage of ammunition. In February the Quartermaster-General had put out what he called 'a looting party' for the benefit of the 3rd Cork Brigade, and Collins had helped in the process. A few days later Liam Lynch of the 2nd Cork Brigade told Collins that they would soon be in a very bad way for rifle ammunition, as they had not been capturing so much recently. 'A few rifles', too, were required at once.

Collins got in touch with Mac Eoin immediately he was arrested and followed him through every stage of his imprisonment. He tried to effect an escape for him from the King George V Military Hospital in Dublin, and, when that failed, he conceived a most daring plan to rescue him from Mountjoy.[12] Five men from the Squad seized an armoured car on the North Circular Road, killing its occupants, and took aboard Emmet Dalton, the Assistant Director of Training, wearing the army uniform he had worn on the Somme in 1918, and Joe Leonard, similarly attired. The guard at the prison opened the gate to them, and the two 'British' officers had actually arrived in the governor's office when shots fired in the yard below denoted that an alarm had been raised. They got back to the armoured car and out of the prison, but without Mac Eoin.

Collins continued his efforts, and as the date of Mac Eoin's trial on the charge of killing a police inspector drew near he arranged with the solicitor, Michael Noyk, to bring a couple of revolvers to his client with which to fight his way out of the court. That proved impossible, and Mac Eoin, found guilty and sentenced to death, was returned to Mountjoy to await execution.

The papers Mulcahy left behind him when he made his midnight escape caused something of a sensation on being examined in Dublin Castle. They gave evidence of 'a really big, determined and fairly well-organised conspiracy', and of plans for putting out of action the entire electricity plant of Manchester city and for the destruction of all English shipping in Liverpool docks. Brigadier-General Winter noted with pleasure that orders were being issued to the Volunteers to attack in future in large numbers, small attacks having proved a failure. 'Sooner or later', he observed, 'we ought to be able really to drop on a big lot more easily than a small one and give it a proper hiding.' This policy change originated with de Valera, who, on returning from the United States, had expressed anxiety about the military situation. Outside Ireland many of the attacks were being interpreted as 'small incidents or murders', he said — the shooting of a policeman here or there was bad for their reputation — and he propounded the idea of occasional larger actions in which up to five hundred men might be involved.

A decision was thus taken to burn down the Dublin Custom House, and the GHQ staff gave it their blessing, but they were not very keen on it and played no part in planning the operation. It remained a Dublin Brigade affair and 'Collins's outfit' kept out of it, though the Squad and the Active Service Unit were reluctantly allowed to lend a hand *outside* the building.[13] This operation in May 1921 was perhaps the biggest of the whole war; and it paid dividends, political and propagandist, in spectacularly immobilising a building which contained the Local Government Board and a number of minor departments and tax offices. From the IRA angle, however, it was disastrously mismanaged,[14] and to have repeated it would have been catastrophic. Six men were killed, twelve wounded, and about seventy captured, among them some of the best fighting material in the Dublin area, including men from the Squad and the Active Service Unit. Volunteers were so thin on the ground that a diversion, enabling the captured men to escape, could not be improvised. Not surprisingly, therefore, a policy of 'small jobs' was reverted to and 'proved effective, having a marked political and psychological effect on the British which was documented in a series of pessimistic military memoranda in May and June. The official mind had more or less reached its sticking-point.'[15]

On the day following the burning of the Custom House Collins's Finance Department at 22 Mary Street was raided, and, to Winter's great delight, among the documents found was a letter in which Collins said that 'It was a bloody business that we lost all those gallant fellows yesterday.' The pressure was being piled on. 'I may tell you between ourselves', Collins told de Valera, 'that the escape of Thursday was nothing to four or five escapes I have had since.

They ran me very close for quite a good while on Sunday evening.'

One Saturday afternoon in this period he kept an appointment to meet Sergeant Maurice McCarthy of the Belfast RIC in Kirwan's. McCarthy was having a drink on his own when the pub was raided. He produced his gun and identity pass to the Auxiliaries, who then moved further down the bar and searched Collins and Thornton. As they did so the Auxiliaries were covered from behind the counter by an assistant who had a fully loaded ·45 revolver and would have used it had an attempt been made to take Collins away.[16] Mulcahy, like Collins, was being hotly pursued. Three places he used as offices were raided, causing him to feel that the enemy was 'very close on the heels of some of us'. Was there a traitor in the camp? Collins suspected that there was, and he ferreted around until he discovered who it was. Information had been passed for reward, with a guarantee that no personal harm would befall Collins himself.

2

Another letter found among Collins's papers caused 'a nasty little breeze' in the Castle: it was from Desmond FitzGerald, the Dáil Director of Publicity, giving an account of an interview between Erskine Childers, the acting Director, then briefly held in custody, and Alfred W. Cope, the Assistant Under-Secretary in Dublin Castle. The letter noted Cope's pacific attitude at a time when British Intelligence had reason to believe they were getting on top of the situation. 'Andy' Cope had been working in the Castle for about a year by now. An assistant secretary in the Ministry of Pensions and formerly a customs detective, he had made an inspection of the Irish departments for the head of the Treasury, one result of which was the weeding out of some senior officials from the Chief Secretary's Office. One man who escaped this process was the Under-Secretary and Privy Councillor, James MacMahon, an influential Catholic who had many avowed Sinn Féiners among his nationalist friends. Cope returned to Ireland soon afterwards with the Chairman of the Board of Inland Revenue, Sir John Anderson, who, sharing a common rank with MacMahon, was to 'administer' Ireland. Cope worked to secret instructions from the Prime Minister, who never hesitated, however, to disavow Cope's actions whenever it was convenient to do so.[17] Cope's job primarily was to establish common ground for negotiations; and, with MacMahon and the Law Adviser, William E. Wylie, he worked towards that end fearlessly and with ultimate success. The trio constituted a 'peace party' within the Castle.

There were many other peacemakers in the field, among them Lord Derby and General Smuts, the Prime Minister of South Africa, with whom de Valera, whose hiding place was known to the British, had meetings that were arranged through Cope. From a secret instruction, intercepted and passed to Collins, it was evident that the British desired to abandon the reprisals policy and terrorist tactics generally. 'It was considered highly desirable on political grounds to endeavour to improve relations with the inhabitants.' Whether by this time Collins had met Cope is uncertain, but messages from Cope were reaching him through the prisoners in Mountjoy, to whom Cope, like Collins, had ready access.

A man who did meet Collins about this time, and in extraordinary circumstances, was William Young Darling, who in later years became a member of parliament and Provost of Glasgow University. He was on the staff of Major-General Tudor, the government's Police Adviser, and was living, far from happily, in the Castle. One day he went to Newry to [82] investigate a collision between a police car and one carrying a number of civilians from Belfast in the company of a high official. He did whatever was necessary and invited the civilians to return to Dublin with him in his chauffeur-driven car. One of these stayed with Darling in front, and, feeling something against his side, he asked Darling if he was carrying a gun. Darling admitted that he was, which led to a guessing game about their respective identities in the course of which the civilian said 'quite simply and very agreeably: "I am Michael Collins."' To this Darling, understandably astounded, could only respond by asking if that meant that he was the Michael Collins the police had made famous. Collins laughed and jestingly allowed the conversation to turn to a variety of indifferent subjects. When they got to a hotel on one of Dublin's squares — Vaughan's possibly — Collins invited Darling in and they had a drink together. 'Collins was an interesting, indeed a fascinating man,' in Darling's opinion. 'He was unarmed, and at his request I put my little pistol on the bar counter.' They discussed books, Von Lettow-Vorbeck on the South-West African guerrilla campaign, Walt Whitman's *Leaves of Grass* and G. K. Chesterton's *Napoleon of Notting Hill*. And they had some political argument before Darling left 'with some feelings of understanding and comprehension'.[18]

3

Things came to a head in June. De Valera, tiring of the efforts that were being made to do business through intermediaries, made it known that a written communication to him would receive a reply; and the form of this was probably being considered when, by sheer accident, de Valera was arrested. He was quickly released, however, minus his papers. He then received a letter from Lloyd George inviting him to London to discuss the possibility of a settlement. The invitation was made in the spirit of a speech, tailored to the ideas of General Smuts, that King George had made at the opening of the parliament of Northern Ireland on 22 June. It was accepted, and to enable it to be fruitful a truce, operative from 11 July, was formally agreed, General Macready, Colonel Brind and 'Andy' Cope signing for the British army and, on 'behalf of the Irish army', Eamon Duggan and Robert Barton.

A checkmate situation appeared to have been reached. Macready, the British Commander-in-Chief, believed that Sinn Féin recognised that their rebellion was about to be crushed and that their future was well-nigh desperate. This may seem a rather exaggerated view, but there is enough evidence to show that Irish morale had declined, that Volunteer strengths had been markedly eaten into by imprisonment and internment, and that in rural areas the urgent need for a superior intelligence system had not been adequately understood.[19] On the other hand, the British government had been driven into a corner politically and morally. The Black and Tan policy had boomeranged against them in Britain and across the world; their civil administration in Ireland had been crippled; and to develop the military campaign into an outright war against the Irish people could not be contemplated until it was first demonstrated that they were incapable of responding to the offer of a generous settlement.

Collins described the situation as he saw it at this time in typically realistic terms:

We took as much of the government of Ireland out of the hands of the enemy as we could, but we could not grasp all of it because he used the whole of his forces to prevent us doing so, and we were unable to beat him out of the country by force of arms. But neither had he beaten us. We had made Ireland too uncomfortable for him. There were too many ambush positions in country areas, and too many gloomy street corners in Cork and Dublin. The British had not surrendered and had no need to agree to humiliating terms any more than we would have done. It was a time for a settlement that would secure for us their withdrawal and evacuation. There was duress, of course. On their side, the pressure of world opinion to conform their practice to their professions, to make an honourable peace with us. On our side, the duress the weaker nation suffers against the stronger, the duress to accept really substantial terms.

These words were spoken after really substantial terms had been accepted. In the interim there was the truce that, initially, was not expected to last and which was seen by the IRA as an opportunity to organise and train and to obtain arms and ammunition.

Collins at an earlier stage had said that 'Without guns you might as well be dead.' Now the emphasis was on the lack of ammunition. 'Ammunition was our most serious problem,' a divisional commandant declared. 'I don't think we ever possessed as much as an average of thirty rounds per rifle. Captured ammunition was, of course, shared out at once, and a fight in which no ammunition was captured was, in effect, a calamity.'[20] That was a widely held view. 'How many rounds did you use?' the head of the Squad would ask anxiously after an operation. And when he was told, 'God blast you!' he would say. 'Could you not have managed with less?'[21] Frank Thornton, who was very close to Collins, recalls the continual difficulties caused by scarcity; and the loss of one of their bomb factories was a bad blow.

The truce came, Thornton said, with dramatic suddenness. A big operation had been planned to wipe out in one blow every enemy agent in the city — this was to have been something vastly bigger than the 'Bloody Sunday' affair — and men from the Dublin Brigade, the Active Service Unit, the Squad and the intelligence corps were actually in their designated attacking positions when, one half-hour before the appointed time, an order to cancel the operation was received from the Dáil cabinet. 'Whether the truce was a good thing or not', Thornton added, 'remains for historians to record, but, in my humble opinion, had it not taken place we would have found ourselves very hard set to continue the fight with any degree of intensity owing to that very serious shortage of ammunition, because men, no matter how determined they may be or how courageous, cannot fight with their bare hands.'[22]

'When we were told of the offer of a truce', Collins is said to have remarked to Sir Hamar Greenwood, 'we were astounded. We thought you must have gone mad.' Mulcahy agreed. To drive the British forces from anything more substantial than a police barracks was beyond them. They recognised the danger, too, of entering into a truce. 'Once a truce is agreed', Collins said, 'and we come out into the open, it is extermination for us if the truce should fail. . . . We shall be . . . like rabbits coming out from their holes.'[23]

5

Negotiating with the Enemy

1

De Valera, with three members of his cabinet, Griffith, Stack and Barton, went to London on 12 July 1921, and, at the close of some amiable conversations, Lloyd George presented a set of proposals, based on dominion status, which provided that the partition of the country enshrined in the Government of Ireland Act would continue; that Britain would maintain control of the seas around Ireland; would have recruiting and air facilities; that the Irish would bear a share of the national debt and war pensions; and would undertake not to impose tariff barriers against Britain. To enable Dáil Éireann to consider these proposals all imprisoned members were released on 6 August with the exception of Mac Eoin. Collins, supported by the Dáil, insisted, however, that there would be no discussion without Mac Eoin. The Longford commandant was accordingly released the same day and was available on 26 August to propose the re-election of de Valera — this time expressly as President of the Irish Republic — doing so in a little speech in Irish that Collins wrote out for him.

The Dáil rejected the British proposals, but, the anxiety for a settlement remaining, a long series of written communications passed backwards and forwards across the Irish Sea until it was agreed to explore 'how the association of Ireland with the community of nations known as the British Empire can best be reconciled with Irish national aspirations'. This formula for a treaty of association pointed to a compromise. The British had made it clear that they would not concede a republic in any

shape or form, and insisted on a form of allegiance to
the Crown. If an agreement was to be achieved, it
would have to contain these constituents. On the
Irish side 'national aspirations' had replaced 'the
Republic', though de Valera hoped to achieve an
approximation to a republican position by working
on the offer of dominion status.

With a formula, or broad terms of reference, agreed,
a conference with the British was set up, and Griffith
introduced an Irish delegation to the first meeting
in London on 11 October 1921. There were no hand-
shakes. Apart from Griffith, the delegation consisted
of Collins, Barton, Duggan and Gavan Duffy. Griffith,
Collins and Barton were drawn from the Dáil cabinet
of seven; of the other four cabinet ministers, Brugha
and Stack refused to go to London, Cosgrave does
not appear to have been asked, and de Valera insisted
on staying behind 'as a symbol of the Republic',
casting his vote, with Brugha, Stack and Barton,
against Griffith, Collins and Cosgrave, who had
argued at great length that he should go.[1] Griffith
and Collins gave their agreement to be part of the
delegation with marked hesitation. Outside the
cabinet meeting, but in the presence of Brugha and
Stack, Griffith, when asked would he go, is reported
to have said to de Valera: 'You are my Chief, and if
you tell me to go, I'll go. But I know, and you know,
that I can't bring back the Republic.' At this point,
allegedly, de Valera produced the concept of 'external
association', the first Griffith had heard of it. The
idea was discussed at some length, and Brugha gave a
reluctant consent to it, while Stack remained silent.
After Brugha and Stack had left, de Valera explained
to Griffith by means of a diagram that the purpose
of his proposal was to reach the republic by degrees,
avoiding the strait-jacket situation into which they
had got themselves, while at the same time bringing

Brugha along.[2] This exposition of what happened and [88] the 'strait-jacket' reference were to be disputed later.

De Valera insisted on Collins going to London and told the Dáil why: 'It was from the personal touch and contact I had with the mind of the Minister of Finance that I felt I knew that he was absolutely vital to the delegation.' Collins disagreed. He was an unknown quantity to the British government, he said, was supposed to represent the extreme or irreconcilable section, and by keeping him at home his name could be played as a card in the game. To send him to London was to place all the Irish cards on the table.[3] He had apparently wanted to go to London on the occasion of de Valera's earlier reconnoitring visit; but the situation was different now in that detailed negotiations were to start with the British rejecting the Republican claim. He felt in his bones that membership of the delegation involved becoming a scapegoat. The task was therefore a loathsome one, but he accepted it 'in the spirit of a soldier who acts against his judgment at the orders of a superior officer'. 'I will never forget his agony of mind,' said Batt O'Connor when Collins visited him the next day. 'He would not sit down, but kept pacing up and down the floor, saying that he should not be put in that position. It was an unheard of thing that the soldier who had fought the enemy in the field should be elected to carry out negotiations. It was de Valera's job, not his.'[4] By contrast, the British Prime Minister would lead his own formidable team.

Griffith's health being far from robust, he asked Collins in London to act as the unofficial leader of the delegation. This Collins did, and carried as much of the burden of the conference as he possibly could. It was an unhappy delegation from the outset, containing within itself the elements of unresolved tension that existed within the cabinet. Collins had always been a most loyal 'Dev' man, but a suspicion of a plot on de Valera's part had entered his mind. Had a trap been set to destroy Griffith and himself? 'I was warned', he told John O'Kane, an Irish businessman-friend living in Hampstead, 'more times than I can recall about the ONE. And when I was caught for this delegation my immediate thought was of how easily I had walked into the preparations. But having walked in, I had to stay.'[5] De Valera's latest biographers say that this suspicion was quite un-justified, though de Valera's feelings towards Collins, and his confidence in him, were not what they had been.[6] Collins had sensed a change when de Valera, at the height of the War of Independence, had wanted to send him to America.

The One, assuming that de Valera was the One, had gone about the selection of the delegation and the laying of a grand strategy for the London talks with great deliberation. That is clear from a quite astonish-ing letter 'for your own eyes only' which he sent to the Irish-American leader Joe McGarrity. He explained that in choosing Griffith and Collins he was anticipating that in a settlement both of them would accept the Crown; and he had chosen Barton because he believed that, backed by his cousin Erskine Childers, 'an intellectual republican' and the delegation's secretary, he would be strong and stubborn enough to act as a retarding force against any precipitate giveaway — by Griffith and Collins no doubt. He intended that 'the cabinet at home should hang on to the delegation's coat-tails', leaving everything safe for a final 'tug-of-war'. He had told the Dáil that the delegates were going to London to do the best they could for the Irish nation, which was how he interpreted his own oath of allegiance to the Republic, and he warned that they were sending men to do what a mighty army and navy could not do, meaning presumably that having failed to beat the British in the field, it remained to be seen what could be achieved by negotiation; but he relied on Barton and Childers to keep the Republican case to the fore-front, and this they would have to do in the absence of Brugha and Stack. However, as de Valera informed McGarrity, even if Brugha or Stack had been prepared to go to London, he would not have chosen them anyhow, for Brugha would have wasted the delega-tion's time in wrangling, and Griffith and Collins would not work with Stack. Two men that he did select, Duggan and Duffy, were dismissed by him as mere legal padding. Duggan, he believed, would follow Collins — almost blindly — while Duffy was more likely to be on the Childers—Barton side.[7] Cosgrave, whom he had not chosen, be dismissed later as 'a ninny'.[8]

From the outset the tension within the delegation that de Valera felt he had provided for was only too evident. It worried Collins and Griffith greatly. They did not know whether they were being instructed or confused,[9] and Griffith felt obliged on one occasion to take a stand against attempts from Dublin to tie the delegation's hands: they were, after all, supposed to be plenipotentiaries. 'The real problem of Dublin' for Collins was the question of trust. 'Who should one trust — even on my own side of the fence?' he asked. Not 'the unmentionables', by whom he must have meant Brugha and Stack especially.

He never lost his affectionate regard for Brugha,[10] but he knew that this was not reciprocated. Brugha disliked Collins's manner, but even more he distrusted his IRB associations; and on one occasion, supported by Stack, he alleged that Collins had mishandled moneys sent to Scotland for the purchase of arms. There was probably nothing more to this than that agents required to have ready money when trying to buy arms from British soldiers, and that Collins was probably unable to impose a strict system of account- ing on some of these disbursements. Brugha, however, insisted on pursuing the matter to the point of calling a full meeting of the GHQ staff to discuss it, and this at a time when the Chief of Staff would not allow more than three members to meet for fear of arrest. Mulcahy protested to de Valera, but got no satisfaction: all de Valera would say was that it was terrible that a good man like Brugha should fall a victim to a dirty little vice like jealousy.[11]

Stack had other reasons for being ill-disposed to Collins. GHQ had twice organised a police force for him in his capacity as Minister for Home Affairs, but it had twice 'melted in his hands', leaving Collins and Mulcahy to conclude that they were dealing with 'a dud'.[12] Then, brutally outspoken as he often was, Collins, in the presence of others, told Stack that his Department of Home Affairs was 'a bloody joke', leaving letters unanswered and causing people to turn to the Department of Finance in the expectation that Collins somehow would see to it that replies were sent.

Erskine Childers became involved in the conflict of personalities. He had joined the movement under Barton's influence and had impressed Collins at their first meeting. Collins introduced him to de Valera, who, greatly attracted to the man, set him to work under Desmond FitzGerald on the production of a news and propaganda bulletin. Originally an English Liberal, Childers had written a book on the Home Rule Bill of 1912 in which he had treated Irish secession as out of the question; later, in 1914, he and his wife had played an important part in the Howth gunrunning. In an intermission from war service he had worked on the secretariat of the Irish Convention of 1917–18 and was accepted as an authority on forms of self-government. In appointing him secretary to the delegation to the London conference, de Valera had acted without Griffith's approval; and he availed of Childers's services when preparing the draft of the document, later known as Document No. 2, which was intended as a guide to the principles the delegation could accept, the primary one being that of external association. Of Childers it has been said, perhaps exaggeratedly, that his attachment to the Irish cause had hardened into an intense fanatical republicanism.[13] All things considered, he was clearly more of a liability than an asset to the negotiating parties. The British disliked him. To them he was a turncoat, a mischief-maker, and the most extreme individual on the Irish side. Some of them thought that he was on the edge of a breakdown, overwrought, 'logical', and so given to introducing qualifications into documents that it was considered highly desirable to keep him off committees in order that business might proceed more expeditiously. Among his critics, Griffith complained of a 'damned Englishman' interfering in Irish affairs; Collins saw him as a watchdog for 'Dublin', sending reports that were masterpieces of the half-statement and painting a picture that was far from the true state of things. He should have been the delegation's leader and not its secretary — that, at any rate, was how he was behaving.

'Who then do I trust?' Collins asked, and he answered by saying: 'Beyond Griffith, no one.' There was Duggan, of course, but he leaned on Collins so much that he could be said to be his *alter ego*. The conference had brought Griffith and Collins closer together than they had ever been, so close that they could exchange intimate confidences. 'You realise what we have on hands,' Griffith said one day, meaning the 'Dublin' reaction to whatever they brought off. Collins replied that he had long realised this, and, looking at 'the good man' whose declining health spoke of a life spent in trial and trouble, he told him how when young he had thought of Griffith as Ireland. 'We stand or fall in this together,' Griffith then said; and that, for Collins, was 'the one bright hope in all the welter of action and counter-action'.

2

Most of the action and counter-action occurred as the Irish delegation faced, either in full conference, sub-conference, or committee, day after day, week after week, from October to December, the team Lloyd George had assembled from among his coalition colleagues and whose strength could be gauged from the fact that Winston Churchill occupied fourth place in it. It was supported by an extremely able group of civil servants, among them 'Andy' Cope of the Dublin Castle administration and Tom Jones of the cabinet secretariat, both of whom were on the easiest of personal terms with the Prime Minister and who, often on their own initiative, contrived to smooth out difficulties. The actual negotiators had ample time to size each other up. In a dossier supplied by the British Civil Service to Birkenhead, the Lord Chancellor, the 'impetuous and rather excitable' Collins, whose influence, it was anticipated, would be exercised on the side of moderation, was seen as the strongest personality on the Irish side, and Griffith the real power. Barton had no outstanding quality. Duggan was completely under the influence of Collins, and Gavan Duffy was vain and self-sufficient and liked to hear himself talk. In independent judgments after the negotiations began, Cope told his Dublin Castle colleagues that Collins showed frankness and considerable reasonableness, while Macready said that Collins was proving a great disappointment, flippantly trying to get out of corners by poor jokes

in bad taste. Griffith, he though, was the strong
silent man.[14]

Collins viewed the British negotiators as 'a nest of singing-birds'. They chirruped mightily one to the other, but the falseness of it all was obvious: they did not trust each other. Birkenhead, Carson's 'galloper' in 1914, who still loomed in the Irish imagination as a sinister, even satanic power,[15] was the best of them, and the negotiations would have been much easier had his colleagues shared his integrity, courage and capacity for clear thinking. Collins did not like Austen Chamberlain, the Chancellor of the Exchequer, at all, and found the strain of looking into his monocle unnerving: he was 'difficult', never informal, said one thing and meant another, hugged the middle of the road, and probably thought of the Irish as a bunch of heathens. For Sir Hamar Greenwood, the Chief Secretary for Ireland, Collins had nothing but detestation, and he believed that the feeling was reciprocal. A 'no problem' gentleman, Greenwood would settle the issue in one day — in favour of Britain. Collins found it difficult to sum up Churchill, full as he was of the ex-officer jingoistic outlook. He was a politician pure and simple, and on the whole Collins did not trust him. As for Lloyd George, Collins thought he was aptly named the 'Welsh Wizard'. He was shrewd and crafty, and Collins's suspicions of him increased as he noted how his manner of addressing people fluctuated, depending on whether he wished to be fatherly, benevolent or formal; he would address Collins, for instance, as 'Mick', 'Michael' or plain 'Mr Collins'. He would sell his nearest and dearest for political gain, and Collins had no doubt that, for reasons of personal prestige, he desperately needed to bring the conference to a successful conclusion. What Lloyd George thought of Collins varied from time to time. While the fighting in Ireland was going on he appeared to have had a secret admiration for him, regretting that his services had not been available to the British during the Great War. He would have been worth a dozen brass hats. But in 1922 he would speak of Collins as a wild animal, a mustang.

In the welter of action and counter-action Collins was uncomfortably aware of the growth, while the conference proceeded, of 'a certain state of lawlessness' in the ranks of the Volunteers at home, making them 'a prey to any ideas, good or bad, exhibited by any leader or supposed leader'. Recurring breaches of the truce created no end of difficulties for him and drove him to defend infractions that were scarcely defensible; this undoubtedly gave Macready additional grounds for disappointment and complaint.

Ernie O'Malley describes an investigation, conducted by Collins personally, of a raid for arms. Coming over to where Volunteers men suspected of the raid stood,

> He planted his legs apart and thrust his head forward. 'Some of you bloody fellows know about this. The rifles did not walk away. Negotiations in London will be held up over a few rifles. The British will say we have broken faith.' He tossed his hair back from his forehead with a shake of his head. 'Come on, by Christ, and answer the questions I ask.' His voice became threatening. 'We are not going to let you get away with those lousy rifles.' . . . He put his hands deep in his trousers' pockets, lifted himself a little on his feet, came back again on his heels, then turned abruptly, walked out and banged the door.[16]

The lawless situation had begun with eleventh-hour warriors in comparatively peaceful parts of the country hastening to make up arrears by attacking the British a few minutes before the formal cessation of hostilities. These exhibitions of prowess when danger was past introduced a subtle demoralisation that spread during the truce proper. Officers and men in the country, out of touch with larger issues than the guerrilla warfare of their own districts, became affected by hero-worship and began seriously to believe that the British had been beaten into the sea. Men who had been on permanent active service had to be kept on hands, of course, while the talks in London continued; but if they went home, they found it hard to settle into the dull routine work of the farms. Some of them who had behaved splendidly in the face of danger went to pieces when the danger was over. From being models of sobriety they took to hard drinking. They learned to swagger about in trench-coats and leggings, with revolvers in their pockets, and to commandeer motor-cars to take them to any place they wished to go on the plea of IRA business. There was an inrush of new recruits too, and young fellows who had been fearful and timid suddenly became aggressive and warlike.[17] Collins was understandably contemptuous of these 'trucileers' — 'sunshine soldiers' he called them.

There were breaches on the other side too. Griffith read to the London conference a circular issued from British GHQ, intended, he said, to give the military and police the idea that the negotiations would not last long and that when they broke down they must be prepared for a remorseless 'hunting down of rebels'. When Sir Laming Worthington-Evans, the Secretary of State for War, said he did not know that any document had in fact been issued, Collins retorted: '*We* know. You can't issue these documents without my knowledge.' Even then Worthington-Evans disputed that the document was a breach of the truce, whereupon Collins, refusing to be baulked, recalled that the British had circulated a photograph of himself for police purposes and that a British detective, by no accident, had come to watch him at Mass.

3

During those months in London Collins had to resist efforts to patronise and lionise him. He did this rather successfully by accepting very few invitations to people's houses. He chose his own company when he went to the theatre, to see, for example, the revival of *The Beggar's Opera,* and he invited friends to relax with him in the Hans Place house that, with another in Cadogan Terrace, had been rented for the duration of the conference. He saw a good deal of his sister Hannie, of course, and of John O'Kane, who thought Collins looked ill, aged beyond his years, nervy and unhappy. He revisited old haunts with Sam Maguire and had a parcel of cigarettes and liquor taken from him by an apologetic warder when he went to see Neil Kerr in prison. Through the Llewelyn Davieses he met Sir John and Lady Lavery, Augustus John, and Sir James Barrie, whose writings he had always admired and who, on being introduced, found Collins 'blazing with intelligence'. His acquaintance with Hazel Lavery was an embarrassment. She developed a romantic attachment to him that he was unable and unwilling to share. When he died she draped herself in widow's weeds and had to be restrained from wearing them at the funeral. Worse still, she interpolated passages of her own composition into his letters and showed them around.[18]

Ned Broy, whose release from prison he had secured, stayed with Collins in Hans Place and acted as a personal bodyguard. One morning he went after Collins when he saw him leaving the house early and found him at Mass in Brompton Oratory. Collins was furious when he discovered that he had been followed, but he saw the point when Broy reminded him of the purpose for which he had been brought over. Going to Mass on weekdays was not something Collins did regularly. He was not pious in that sense, but when faced with serious difficulties, as he now was, he would turn to his faith for guidance and support. He carried a relic of St Paul about with him and used to explain that Paul, like himself, had not always been as good as he should have been, and that, like himself also, he had been in many a tight corner. There was always the danger that someone would try to kill Collins in revenge for the many assassinations with which his name was popularly linked, and for that reason Broy was intermittently joined by some of Collins's 'gunmen': Liam Tobin, Tom Cullen, Emmet Dalton and Joe Dolan among them. On them Collins perpetrated the schoolboy pranks he loved to play, pulling them out of bed in the morning or stealing their bedclothes.

There were times, though there cannot have been many, when he felt lonely and walked the streets by himself, with Broy somewhere in the rear, no doubt. He confessed as much to Kitty Kiernan, the lovely girl from Granard whose acquaintance he had made during the South Longford by-election in 1917 and intended to marry. They can hardly have had much opportunity for courtship: he was so immersed in his numerous activities that he was sometimes called away from her side and had to rely on a colleague to look after her. He sent her notes from London; but when he sat down to write one of these he noticed that it was already four in the morning and he had to be in Downing Street at ten. He tried to keep in touch with what was going on at home by going over at weekends: and he once managed to get down to a training camp in West Cork, fitting in a visit to his family and taking a turn in the fields. He maintained regular contact with the Supreme Council of the IRB, who, for him, were the touchstone of national feeling, kept them informed about the progress of the negotiations and sought their views on critical issues.[19]

4

One issue he must somehow have touched on was that of dominion status. It had become the vital issue, the sole alternative to the Republic on which agreement with the British was likely to be reached. His mind was full of it, and he had been studying the authorities — Duncan Hall, Berridale Keith, Josiah Wedgwood and Jan Smuts. In a 'personal and unofficial' memorandum for some members at least of the British delegation, Collins indicated the position his thinking had reached on the subject of Ireland as a prospective member of the British Commonwealth and foreshadowed the Statute of Westminster of 1931 which declared the equality in status of Britain and the dominions alike, that in no way were they subordinate one to another in any aspect of their domestic or external affairs.

The Colonies as full-grown children [Collins wrote] are restive under any appearance of parental restraint, though willing to co-operate with the parent on an equal footing in regard to all family affairs. Ireland, as a separate nation, would be also restive under any control from the neighbouring nation, but equally willing to co-operate in free association on all matters . . . of common concern. . . . The problem on both sides can only be solved by recognising without limitation the complete independence of the several countries, and only on that basis can they all be associated by ties of co-operation and friendship. The only association which it will be satisfactory for Ireland to enter will be based, not on the present technical legal status of the Dominions, but on the real position they claim, and have in fact secured. It is essential that the *de facto* position should be recognised *de jure,* and that all its implications as regards sovereignty, allegiance and constitutional independence should be acknowledged. An association on the foregoing conditions would be a novelty in the world. But the world is looking for such a development.

Writing to Lord Birkenhead, Austen Chamberlain described this document as 'extraordinarily interesting though sometimes perverse and sometimes Utopian. Who (outside our six [members of the delegation]) would guess the name of the writer?'[20]

5

Collins was in Dublin on 25 November for a cabinet meeting, which, beginning at three o'clock, was still in progress at seven when Mulcahy and his general staff, who had been waiting since five, were called in to discuss a matter of which Brugha had given notice three weeks earlier. This was a matter fundamentally involving Brugha, Stack and de Valera on the one hand, and Collins on the other in his dual capacity as President of the IRB and member of the GHQ staff of the IRA. In August 1919, as we have seen, the Dáil decided on Brugha's motion, as Minister of Defence, that every Volunteer should swear allegiance to the Republic and the Dáil; in March 1921 it had acknowledged responsibility for the wartime actions of the Volunteers. This assertion of Dáil authority raised a question for men whose prime allegiance had hitherto been to the IRB, and for the IRB itself, of course. With some hesitation the IRB had proceeded to amend its own constitution, ceding to Dáil Éireann the governmental powers of its Supreme Council and disposing, for the time being at any rate, of the claim to constitute the chief executive authority of the Republic.[21] Collins in effect got out of de Valera's way.

To make Dáil control completely effective de Valera now obtained agreement that the government of the Dáil should issue fresh commissions to officers of the army and have an oath administered to all ranks. In pursuance of this, Brugha communicated in writing with the members of the general staff and the commanders of divisions that had been created under a new grouping scheme. His letter spoke of the possibility of further fighting and of the need to put the army in an unequivocal position as the legal defence force of the nation under the control of the civil government. It went on to indicate that 'a new army' was being set up as from the 25 November 1921, the anniversary of the founding of the Volunteers in 1913, and offered to the recipients of the letter a renewal of their positions. Mulcahy was both amused and confused when offered his old post, because, twice since the truce began, Brugha had given him notice of dismissal and instructed him to hand over his papers to Austin Stack, the Deputy Chief of Staff. Mulcahy explains in his papers that in his position as Chief of Staff he had been the channel through which Brugha directed his attacks on Collins. 'I was', he wrote, 'a bad contact for the transmission of these attacks, and in that way Cathal became somewhat antagonistic to myself.' He meant, of course, that he defended Collins, because, despite their very different personalities, Mulcahy and Collins shared a deep sense of trust, harmony and respect for each other. Mulcahy had, moreover, an immense regard for Collins's 'tireless, vigorous, almost turbulent hard work' and for his 'daring' and 'enormous momentum'.[22] This view of Collins was widely shared. Some Volunteer commanders might complain of the inadequacies of GHQ, but their criticisms did not extend to Collins personally. They might wilt at times under his caustic tongue, but they venerated him nonetheless; and the more active they themselves were the more they admired his achievements.[23]

As for handing over his papers to the Deputy Chief of Staff, that was a role in which Mulcahy had difficulty in recognising Stack. At the reconstruction of the Volunteers after the Rising, he had mentioned that he would like to have Stack on the staff and, for want of some definite position for him, suggested that he might be called 'Deputy Chief of Staff'; but Stack had never really functioned in that capacity, and it was widely felt that even his role as Minister for Home Affairs was too much for him. The assignment of multiple functions to individuals had been terribly overdone in any event, though in Collins's case it had worked well. Mulcahy, in addition to being Chief of Staff, was Assistant Minister of Defence and in that capacity had once been told by de Valera that he should attend cabinet meetings. But, quickly changing his mind, de Valera had said: 'No, you would probably be as bad as the rest of them after a fortnight' – a pointer to the unhappy condition of affairs within the cabinet.[24]

Mulcahy, on being asked for his reaction to the 'new army' idea, expressed the hope that, before the old army was abolished, those who had made it should be thanked for their past services. He would agree to be Chief of Staff in the new set-up, provided he was allowed to select and appoint the staff. This produced some acrimony, for Mulcahy wanted Eoin O'Duffy to be his Deputy Chief, whereas Brugha had earmarked the job for Stack. The discussion had reached the point where de Valera was suggesting as a compromise that O'Duffy could act as Deputy Chief for Mulcahy and that Stack could be 'Brugha's ghost on the staff' when Griffith and Collins had to leave to catch the mail boat for the long and tiring journey back to London.

The other headquarters officers waiting in the ante-room were then admitted, and de Valera, having explained that he wanted to reform the staff, asked them what they thought of the idea. One by one they rejected it, and 'Ginger' O'Connell, the Director of Training, appeared to be speaking for them all when he said that the old staff had been a band of brothers and should not be changed. This was a remarkable statement in relation to Collins, for it meant that his colleagues did not feel put out by the pre-eminence among them he had acquired or by his habit of invading their territory whenever it suited him to do so.

When it came to O'Duffy's turn to address the ministers, he, in a shrill voice, characterised the proposed scheme as a meditated insult and a criticism of himself. This upset de Valera. Rising excitedly, he pushed away the table in front of him and, half-screaming, half-shouting, said: 'Ye may mutiny if you like, but Ireland will give me another army,' and dismissed them all from his sight.[25] When calm returned, it must then have dawned on de Valera and Brugha that to attempt to reorganise the GHQ staff against their wishes, and at the most crucial moment of the London negotiations, would be madness. At any rate it was made known a few days later that no new army was to be formed, but that the commissions offered should be formally accepted. That, apparently, was the last that was heard of the matter.[26]

6

Collins and Lloyd George discussed the possible outcome of the London conference when they next met. The Welshman was determined that whatever happened he personally would not be disadvantaged. 'I've got my political life at stake,' he said, a statement to which Collins made no response, though he felt that in his own case it was not his political life only that was at stake.[27] Whatever was to happen to him personally, acceptance of a treaty with Britain would be denounced in Ireland as a gross betrayal, an act of treachery.[28]

On 2 December the full Dáil cabinet assembled in the Dublin Mansion House for what was to be their final opportunity for reviewing the situation. The discussion lasted seven hours. Some of the members — Collins among them — were physically tired even before the meeting began. The night crossing had taken twelve hours, the mailboat having to return to Holyhead after a collision with a fishing smack in which three lives were lost. There was a document before the meeting embodying the position reached in the negotiations; and a clear division became apparent when the individual delegates were asked to state their views. Griffith and Duggan were unhesitatingly in favour of accepting what roughly was on offer. Barton and Duffy were not. Collins, substantially agreeing with Griffith and Duggan, thought that non-acceptance involved a gamble, for Britain could resume the war within a week. He defended what had been done regarding Ulster, believed further concessions could be obtained on trade and defence, favoured giving the country an opportunity of declaring on the treaty that was being formulated, but would not recommend a proposed oath of allegiance. In an earlier exploration of the issues with Griffith he had come to the firm conclusion that the advantages of dominion status to Ireland as a stepping-stone to complete independence were immeasurable, and he recognised that in achieving that status some form of oath was unavoidable. But Childers, whose opinion was also sought — much, no doubt, to Griffith's disgust — spoke of the draft treaty giving Ireland no national status and said that when England went to war she would bring Ireland with her.

At that point, apparently, Brugha intervened with a comment on the obvious split in the delegation: he wanted to know who was responsible for singling out Griffith and Collins to do most of the work, leaving the others without full information. He was told that the British liked it that way but that the whole of the Irish delegation approved of the arrangement. Brugha was not satisfied. What the British had done, he said, was deliberately to pick the weakest men on the Irish side. The remark caused a sensation, and Griffith, leaving his seat, walked over to Brugha and demanded that it be withdrawn. This Brugha stubbornly refused to do, though he subsequently relented.

Much later, according to the Dáil record, it was decided unanimously that the oath, drafted though it was in the form and practice of Canada, could not be subscribed to. The delegation was to return to London and say that the cabinet would not accept the oath if not amended and would face the consequences, but this was not stated to have been an unanimous decision. Griffith was to inform Lloyd George that the proposed articles of agreement could not be signed, to state that the matter was now one for the Dáil, and 'to try and put the blame on Ulster'. De Valera, in the course of the day, in a spoken paraphrase, suggested a form of oath which solemnly swore 'true faith and allegiance to the constitution of the Irish Free State [the designation of the entity that was to replace the Republic], to the Treaty of Association [in the form to be negotiated], and to recognise the King of Great Britain as head of the Associated States [which in the paper known as Document No. 2 were described as 'the States of the British Commonwealth']'. But neither Brugha nor Stack showed interest.

When the delegation arrived back in London, after what the British understood was a 'confused and inconclusive discussion',[29] they were at odds as to how they were to proceed. Perhaps basing their decision on the implications of the oath in the form drawn up by de Valera, Barton and Duffy were convinced that they were to make another attempt to obtain external association. With Childers, therefore, they prepared a memorandum of counter-proposals, the leading heads of which some of the British delegation at least had already seen, but Griffith, Collins and Duggan together refused to present it. Rather than that Barton and Duffy should do it alone, however, Griffith went with them to Downing Street; but Collins refused to budge: he was '"fed up" with the muddle';[30] and the British, when they looked at the memorandum, recognised that it was substantially a return to the external association idea which they had already emphatically rejected, so that no progress whatever was made on foot of it. Like Collins, the British were also getting 'fed up' and were considering calling off the negotiations. A paper was actually in draft stating that after five months of negotiation and nearly two months of conference, in the course of which with the utmost patience the British ministers had searched for any clue that could lead to a settlement, the Irish had nothing to offer but proposals which could break the Empire in pieces, dislocate society in all its self-governing nations, and cancel for ever the hope of national unity in Ireland itself.

Then came a dramatic change. 'Andy' Cope, who

had reflected the general belief that 'all was over, and the conference finished', suddenly felt that the tide had begun to turn.[31] The change, it is now evident, began when Tom Jones of the British cabinet secretariat was alone with Griffith for an hour at midnight on 4–5 December. Griffith, said Jones, was labouring under a deep sense of crisis and spoke throughout with the greatest earnestness and unusual emotion. One was bound to feel that to break with him would be infinitely tragic. He had said that he and Collins had been won over to the belief in Lloyd George's desire for peace and recognised that he had gone far in his efforts to secure it. This belief was not shared by their Dublin colleagues, who still greatly distrusted and feared that if the Treaty was signed, they would be 'sold'. They were being told that they had surrendered much ('the King' and 'association') and had got nothing to offer the Dáil in return. He then made an earnest appeal to Lloyd George that the Northern Ireland Prime Minister, Sir James Craig, should be induced to give a conditional recognition, however shadowy, of Irish national unity in return for the acceptance of the Commonwealth by Sinn Féin, an act that would involve a form of oath satisfactory to the British. They would give all the safeguards the North needed and would drop their demand for a Boundary Commission, a most difficult thing to give up. Griffith also asked that Lloyd George should see Collins and have heart-to-heart talk with him.[32] Such a meeting did in fact take place at 9.30 a.m. on 5 December. Collins outlined the Irish difficulties on Ulster, trade, defence and the oath. He found the Prime Minister, who had obviously been impressed by what Jones had reported of his discussion with Griffith, not unfriendly and ready to make concessions so long as the opening clauses of the draft Treaty, retaining the Free State within the Commonwealth, were accepted;

and to this Collins, by implication, agreed.[33]

That afternoon Collins went back to Downing Street with Griffith and Barton and began a discussion on his four points with Lloyd George, Chamberlain, Birkenhead and Churchill. The most difficult and complicated of these was the question of Ulster, and the sub-conference kept returning to it all day long while awaiting a reply from Craig either accepting or rejecting the unity of Ireland. Griffith, as far back as mid-November had, at a private meeting, agreed to the contents of a memorandum by Lloyd George in which it was said that if Ulster did not see her way to accept the principle of an all-Ireland parliament, the British would then propose to create such a parliament but to allow Ulster to remain subject to the imperial parliament for all the reserved services. In that case, however, it would be necessary to revise the boundary, and this might be done by a Boundary Commission which would be directed to adjust the line both by inclusion and exclusion. On the strength of Griffith's adherence to that memorandum and his undertaking, as was said, not to let Lloyd George down, the Conservative members of the British delegation had adopted a certain attitude at a party conference and staked thereon their political future. Griffith now indicated that he still adhered to that agreement — it was the first time Collins and Barton had heard of it — but he argued that it was not unreasonable to require that Craig should reply before the Irish delegation accepted or refused the proposals in the draft Treaty. With this matter in abeyance, the sub-conference turned to consider objections or proposed alterations in the other areas of the draft Treaty, beginning with the oath of allegiance.

On this, progress was brisk. Birkenhead explained that he had received that morning a form of oath on which Collins had been working, and he had made some alterations of his own. In the draft now presented, 'British Commonwealth' was substituted for 'British Empire' at the instance of the Irish, another example, Jones said, of the effort to assimilate words to the susceptibilities of both sides, a process creating a mishmash of legal verbiage that made the oath almost meaningless.[34] (The IRB, incidentally, had played a part in the formulation of Collins's draft. He had brought the oath before the Supreme Council at an early stage and they, considering its form objectionable, had left it to three members — all high-ranking Volunteer officers — to prepare a more satisfactory alternative. This introduced allegiance to the Irish Free State in the first instance and mentioned the King subordinately. When the Secretary of the Council saw the Treaty in its final form he recognised that the changes suggested by the Council had been adopted.)[35]

No point was made at the sub-conference regarding the Irish Free State's military defence force, whose size was not to exceed such proportion of the British establishments as the population of Ireland bore to that of Great Britain; but the restriction on an Irish naval service, other than for revenue and fishery protection purposes, was strongly contested. If an Irish navy were included in the Treaty, Churchill said, the Treaty would never get through the Westminster parliament; the English people would believe that Irish ships would be used against them in time of war. However, the likelihood of Ireland undertaking a share of her coastal defence was accepted, and provison was made in the draft for an inter-governmental review at the end of five years. Collins then took up the article on trade, and the British conceded full fiscal autonomy, Lloyd George agreeing that there should be freedom on both sides to impose any tariffs they liked.

The sub-conference then went back to the Ulster question. No message had come from Belfast, but Griffith said that he personally would sign the Treaty whether Craig accepted the principle of unity or not. He insisted, however, that his colleagues were in a different position in that they were not a party to the promise he had given to Lloyd George, and that it would be unfair to demand acceptance or refusal from them before Craig replied. Lloyd George replied that he always understood that Griffith spoke for the delegation as a whole; in this matter of peace or war each of the plenipotentiary members should sign the Treaty document and undertake to recommend it, otherwise there could be no agreement. He and his colleagues as a body had hazarded their political futures, and the Irish delegation must do likewise and take the same risks. He produced two letters, one of which, he said, he must send that night to Craig. One was a covering letter to the government's proposals for the future relations of Ireland and Great Britain, stating that the Irish delegation had agreed to recommend them for acceptance. The other stated that the Irish delegation had failed to come to an agreement with the government, and that he had, therefore, no proposals to send. A special train and destroyer were ready to convey either letter to Belfast; the Irish had until ten o'clock to make up their minds as to which should go.

The discussion then turned on the length of time to be given to Northern Ireland in which to decide whether to join the Irish Free State or not. The twelve months stipulated in the draft was too long, the Irish argued; within that period life might be made intolerable for the nationalist people of Ulster, and Collins cited recent occurrences in Tyrone, including the support given to the Northern Ireland government by British troops, that had shaken confidence. The period was eventually reduced to one month, though Lloyd George thought the decision ill-advised. However, it did not seem to matter, since Craig was determined — and this Lloyd George knew — to refuse the Treaty terms anyway. It was then agreed to dismiss and reassemble at ten. 'Michael Collins rose,' said Churchill, 'looking as though he was going to shoot someone, preferably himself. In all my life I have never seen so much pain and suffering in restraint.'

It cannot then have been far off nine o'clock. As they sped away from Downing Street, Collins told Griffith that he would join him in signing the Treaty. At Hans Place Duggan said that he too would sign. That left Barton and Duffy to make up their minds. Arthur Griffith's personal secretary, Kathleen MacKenna, takes up the story:

> In Hans Place the typewriters were going full speed. I was in the hall when Collins came in with the intention of joining the other delegates and the secretaries and leaving with them for Downing Street. But at that time the others were in a room upstairs squabbling. Mick went into the dining-room and down to the end of it where there was a bar. Tom, the head waiter, poured him out a glass of port. Mick then plumped down on a chair in such a way that he could see the others as they descended. Then he fell fast asleep. I watched his pale flabby face as he sat there holding in one hand his attaché case and thrown over it his old shabby brown dust coat. I watched them all as they left in the cars for Downing Street. All were silent, taut and serious as if walking in a funeral procession.[36]

Barton and Duffy, after much soul-searching, had decided to follow Griffith's lead and sign. No doubt they, and the others for that matter, adverted to an instruction to refer back to Dublin before signing, but felt that it had been superseded by circumstances.

Griffith, Collins and Barton were back in Downing Street at ten minutes to ten according to Jones, or at a quarter past eleven according to Barton, but both agree that what then occurred kept the two groups together until twenty minutes past two in the following morning. An effort was made, but failed, to remove the clause in the draft Treaty which provided that the Governor-General of Ireland would be appointed in like manner as the Governor-General of Canada; but it was agreed that the title 'Governor-General' could be dropped and replaced by any alternative the Irish preferred other than 'President'. Collins demanded and secured that the Free State's military defence force would not be restricted to being a 'local' force only. Alterations were made consequent on what had earlier been agreed, and the consistently helpful Lord Chancellor did the necessary redrafting. Ordinarily 'a politician of unprincipled and unbridled ambition', Birkenhead could be a good friend and rise to heights of 'self-denying statesmanship'.[37] The mutual respect that had developed between him and Collins enabled him in the negotiations to act, as it were, against his nature. Looking at the political problems the British delegation had to contend with, Churchill, the Liberal, was to say later that the Treaty had only been made possible by the Tory Birkenhead's courage and patriotism: at the critical moment he had been prepared to run all manner of risks with his party, among whom there were diehards who were consumed with bitterness against the settlement.

Lloyd George finally asked whether the Irish as a delegation were prepared to accept the Articles of Agreement and to stand by them in their parliament as the British delegation would stand by them in theirs. Griffith replied affirmatively. Then, having discussed the release of prisoners and the procedure for ratification, the final draft was read over, agreed to and signed; and, for the first time since Lloyd George had introduced them across the table to obviate the need for 'shaking hands with murderers', the British representatives walked round and shook hands with men they had come to respect.[38] 'I was in the hall of Hans Place with Tom, the waiter,' Kathleen MacKenna wrote, 'when he opened the door at their return and they filed into the house. They were serious, sleepy, relaxed. Diarmuid O'Hegarty opened the Treaty and I saw the still fresh signatures. After Duggan and Duffy signed it, Childers rolled it up and went to his office with it. He looked more haggard that evening: he was nervy and irritable.'[39]

When Collins had had a sleep he sat down and wrote a memorable letter to John O'Kane. It tells better than any biographer could what he had been through and what he feared the future had in store for him:

> When you have sweated, toiled, had mad dreams, hopeless nightmares, you find yourself in London's streets, cold and dank in the night air.
>
> Think — what have I got for Ireland? Something which she has wanted these past seven hundred years. Will anyone be satisfied at the bargain? Will anyone? I tell you this — early this morning I signed my death warrant. I thought at the time how odd, ridiculous — a bullet might just as well have done the job five years ago. . . .
>
> These signatures are the first real step for Ireland. If people will only remember that, the first real step.

7

At the earliest possible opportunity the Dáil cabinet

reviewed what had happened in a long, turbulent and unproductive meeting before de Valera repudiated the settlement.[40] Next he and Griffith announced their respective positions to the public; and then on 14 December the Dáil began to consider the issue in a series of meetings, both private and public, that, with a break for Christmas, stretched into the new year. In between times de Valera arranged an interview with the GHQ staff to seek their views and their intentions in the event of his winning the vote against the Treaty. Collins, speaking for himself, indicated that he would continue to serve, but as an ordinary soldier only.[41] The issue appeared simple enough — peace or a resumption of the war, a conceptual republic or positive dominion status — but it was anything but simple for deputies with little political experience who were easily swayed by emotional attachments or other considerations. During the debate Collins asked a friend to 'tally' with him a list of the members so as to forecast the result. A Cork name came up and someone canvassed the side he would take. Collins muttered: '*Against* — dishonestly against.' Then he drew a breath and laughed: 'Or else dishonestly for.'[42]

In the first private meeting Seán Mac Eoin, advocating approval of the Treaty, emphasised what the issue meant in military terms so far as his command was concerned. He had more men than before, four thousand in all, but in the matter of armament the situation was disastrous. He had one rifle for every fifty men, and about as much ammunition as would last them about fifty minutes per rifle. 'When we started operations before', he explained, 'we took particularly good care that nobody knew anything about us, and whatever we did was done by bluff — pure bluff.' The advantage they had had in an intelligence service had been lost during the truce; and if the war restarted, they would be without another invaluable asset, the help and support of the civilian population. Collins had given some similarly stark statistics to an IRB 'circle' of which he was the 'centre'. In the previous June, he told them, the total number of men in Active Service Units was 1,617. They had but one weapon per man, not as much as one cartridge per gun, and their ammunition route had been discovered, so that the truce had come to them as a godsend.

Supporting in the Dáil the motion to approve the Treaty, he insisted that the measure was not being recommended for more than it contained. Equally he did not recommend it for less than it contained. 'In my opinion,' he stated, 'it gives us freedom, not the ultimate freedom that all nations desire and develop to, but the freedom to achieve it.' And Griffith, in turn, spoke as Parnell might have spoken, when he declared that 'the Treaty settlement had no more finality than that they were the final generation on the face of the earth'. The motion was carried on 7 January 1922 by seven votes, and on successive days de Valera resigned as President of the Republic — though this did not appear necessary and the supporters of the Treaty would have preferred him not to have done so — then allowed his name to go forward for re-election and, on being defeated by two votes, walked out of the House with his followers to shouts of 'Deserters all!' from Collins. Griffith was then elected unopposed in his place.

The close voting did not represent the state of public opinion, as became evident to deputies during the Christmas recess. One opponent of the Treaty resigned his seat because he found that his constituents were so solidly for it; and Collins, confident that this reflected the position generally in the country, suggested that the opposition in the Dáil should be withdrawn. It actually became more vociferous. A common cry went up that the Republic was being abandoned, that it was now a case of 'Heads up into the Empire!' On the other hand, the merits of de Valera's Document No. 2, an external association proposal which had emerged as an alternative to the Treaty, were dismissed with references to Tweedledum and Tweedledee.

Accusations of bad faith filled the air: Collins and others who followed his lead were 'traitors'. A woman was reported in the Dáil debate as having said that Collins would be shot if he went to Cork, and if no man would shoot him, she would do it herself. There were allusions to 'slippery slopes', to the 'atmosphere of London', to 'the coalition between Downing Street and the delegation', to Collins 'the Fleet Street hero who was worse than Castlereagh', to the likelihood that he and Griffith had been drunk or drugged when they signed the Treaty. It was even alleged that the King's daughter, Princess Mary, was breaking off her engagement to Lord Lascelles in order to marry Collins, who was to be the first Governor of the Irish Free State. Collins did not think that a particularly funny remark: he rose in the Dáil to protest against the possibility of pain being caused both to the lady mentioned and to the lady to whom he was by now betrothed.

An unusually savage attack was directed against him by one of the many men in the assembly with IRA connections. Séamus Robinson, having introduced a signed declaration against the Treaty from commanders of a number of divisions and brigades, referred to the catchword that 'what was good enough for Mick is good enough for me' and asked on what the expression was based. Griffith, he said, had called Collins 'the man who won the war'; the press had called him 'the Commander-in-Chief of the IRA';

others had described him as a 'great exponent of
guerrilla warfare', and 'the elusive Mike'. But he
(Robinson), the country, aye, and the world wanted
to know what position exactly he held in the Irish
Republican Army; whether he had ever taken part in
any armed conflict; the number of battles he had
been in; in fact was there any authoritative record of
his having ever fired a shot for Ireland? And, as if
that was not enough, Robinson broadly hinted that
Collins and Griffith had signed the Treaty with malice
aforethought and had bluffed and stampeded the rest
of the delegation into signing also. The following
day, in apparent collusion with Robinson, Brugha
answered his questions in a long and bitter speech.
His department, the Department of Defence, was
divided into sections, he explained. One section was
the GHQ staff of the army, and that section was
further divided into sub-sections. 'One of the heads
of the sub-sections is Mr Michael Collins; and to use
a word which he has on more than one occasion used,
and which he is fond of using, he is merely a subordinate in the Department of Defence.'

Although the debate became desperately boring,
with practically every deputy determined to make a
speech that would go down in history, it had the
strange features that Terence de Vere White has
described — much latent hysteria; the calm, courteous
but unsound reasoning of Childers; the restless, sometimes effeminate emotionalism of de Valera; the
moderation of Collins; the firm manliness of Griffith;
the withering blight of Mary MacSwiney; the naïvety
of the other women; the weakness and candour of
Barton; the sterile bitterness of Brugha; the incor-
rigible idealism of Mellows; the cynicism of J. J.
Walsh; and the intelligence of two young men, Kevin
O'Higgins and Patrick Hogan.[43] The firm manliness
of Griffith came across in a speech that Frank

O'Connor rightly described as magnificent oratory: 'It was by far the most effective, reasonable and persuasive in the whole debate.'[44] He touched on Brugha's belittlement of Collins and the rejection of Griffith's statement that Collins was the man who won the war. He stood by that statement. 'Collins', he said, 'was the man who made the situation. He was the man whose matchless and indomitable will carried Ireland through the terrible crisis. He was the man who fought the Black and Tan terror until England was forced to offer terms.' And he added: 'Though I have not now, and never had, an ambition about either political affairs or history, if my name is to go down in history, I want it associated with the name of Michael Collins.'

Before the anti-Treaty deputies departed, Griffith assured de Valera that he would maintain the Republic until the people by their votes settled the Treaty question once and for all; and Mulcahy, Brugha's successor as Minister of Defence, tried to counter the spreading fear of anarchy with a promise that the army would be kept intact. There was absolutely nothing, he said, that should give anybody uneasiness; but time was quickly to reveal how difficult of fulfilment that promise was. The division in the cabinet was repeated in the Army Council — eight members favouring acceptance of the Treaty and three against. Among the field commanders and the rank and file of the army large numbers opposed the Treaty from the start, particularly in the southern counties. In the Supreme Council of the IRB the voting was eleven for, and four, including Harry Boland and Liam Lynch, against; and it was alleged that undue influence had been brought to bear on members who were Dáil deputies. This was denied. The Council had in fact decided that the Treaty should be approved, but that until a draft Free State constitution was available

representatives of Southern Ireland — in effect the pro-Treaty members of Dáil Éireann plus the four Unionist representatives of Dublin University; and two days later Dublin Castle, the centre and symbol of British administration, was formally surrendered to Collins by the Lord Lieutenant, who was attended by Under-Secretary James MacMahon of the 'peace party'. It is not recorded what FitzAlan said on the occasion, but MacMahon very naturally said: 'We're glad to see you, Mr Collins,' to which Collins is said to have replied: 'Like hell you are!' Collins more than once thereafter went to London to arrange details of the transfer with the Colonial Secretary, Winston Churchill. On one occasion the meeting was delayed by Churchill's absence, and by the time he arrived, Collins, with many home worries on his mind, was clearly in a bad humour. Churchill apologised for being late and turned hurriedly to the agenda, the first item on which was the Viceregal Lodge. 'What, Mr Collins,' he asked, 'do you intend doing with the Viceregal Lodge?' 'I think', said Collins, angrily biting out the words, 'we'll make a bloody cancer hospital out of it.'[1]

For a little while the Provisional Government was headquartered in the City Hall, alongside Dublin Castle, before moving into a building in Merrion Street that was almost ready for occupation as an extension of the College of Science. In the same building Griffith established his Dáil Éireann headquarters. The two governments functioned in parallel, though meeting occasionally together when circumstances so demanded. Collins was the important link between them, being, with Cosgrave, Duggan and Kevin O'Higgins, a member of both ministries. The creation of new services and the incorporation of existing ones into the structure of the Provisional Government proceeded without apparent difficulty, but it took up a great deal of Collins's time and deflected him to a degree from the military and political areas where his presence was so important. The evacuation or disbandment of the Crown forces left the IRA the only armed force in the country through which authority could be exercised; but the IRA was not very well qualified for the task. It was a citizen army, an army of men with strong political sentiments who reacted to the Treaty, one way or the other, as violently as the politicians did. For many of them it was no longer a question of following whatever lead the Dáil gave them, but of doing what they could to give effect to their own ideas. And the possibilities of disorder were enhanced, as we have seen already, with so many officers of high rank being members of the Dáil. During the debate on the Treaty all of the six members of the GHQ staff who were also deputies spoke, five for the Treaty, one (Mellows) against; but other members of the staff were also involved, and, on the day following Mulcahy's appointment as Minister of Defence, one of these, Rory O'Connor, supported by Mellows, served a document on him; it carried the signatures of a number of influential officers and called for the immediate holding of an Army Convention. Later O'Connor indicated that, if this were not done, the Convention would be called by the signatories. The difficulty was deferred for a couple of months, during which time anti-Treaty officers throughout the country tightened their grip on the military barracks in their possession that had been handed over by the British and took what opportunity they could to import and accumulate arms and equipment. On the pro-Treaty side initial steps were taken to create a uniformed National Army as well as a uniformed police force. An unsuccessful effort was made to reunite Irish-Americans, on the principle of acquiescence by them in the wishes of the Irish people as constitutionally expressed.

The British followed the situation closely. Early in January Churchill told the Prince of Wales that what he called 'the Irish event' seemed to be going well. Griffith and Collins were men of their word. It used to be said that Irishmen had every form of courage except moral courage, but, in Churchill's opinion, that could be said no longer. He had been given the chairmanship of the cabinet Committee on Irish Affairs, and, full of hope and confidence, he was starting in to get the Provisional Government under way. His optimism quickly evaporated, however. Within a week he was fearing bloody news from Ireland, which would mean that the decision to withdraw troops the moment the Dáil approved the Treaty could not be adhered to. British soldiers had been forcibly disarmed in Co. Cork, and a situation approaching open war had developed on the northern border. In reaction to an anti-Catholic pogrom in which men were driven from their employment, homes burned down, and women and children subjected to terrorism, and in one instance five members of a Belfast family murdered, IRA columns, with direction and arms surreptitiously supplied by Collins in collaboration with Liam Lynch, an uncompromising anti-Treaty IRA commandant, proceeded to make cross-border raids, to disarm police, to take hostages, to block or blow up roads and bridges and seize military material. In Clones railway station on 11 February a party of Special Constables travelling to Enniskillen was attacked, four of them killed, others wounded and sixteen taken prisoner.

Field-Marshal Sir Henry Wilson, about to retire from the army and enter parliament, spoke of reconquest, and Macready wanted to know what he was to do if de Valera proceeded to a *coup d'état* or got a majority in favour of a republic at the elections. In the absence of instructions he intended to declare martial law, to tell the Provisional Government to remain quiescent, and to take complete charge of Dublin. Churchill, however, replied that there was not going to be an independent republic in Ireland. The battle had been joined on that issue by the men with whom they in Britain had signed the Treaty. Collins and Craig came together on a number of occasions between the end of January and the end of March, when a Craig–Collins pact was signed. This promised a lot, but it had little real effect upon the situation, and the violence in the North continued unabated.[2]

The pro-Treaty leaders were not always at one in dealing with difficulties. Griffith would have liked to have forced a vote on the Treaty issue when the Sinn Féin Ard-Fheis reconvened late in February, but the feeling of the meeting was against him, and Collins entered into an agreement with de Valera that the issue should not be put to a vote at all and that the general election should be postponed for three months, by which time the electors would be able to look at the Treaty and the constitution of the Irish Free State together. During those three months the country reeled towards civil war. Sinn Féin remained nationally united, but de Valera formed a new party, and the IRA went to pieces. As March began, Collins was alarmed by the theft from the RIC barracks at Clonmel of a huge stock of rifles, machine-guns and ammunition. Churchill protested to Collins. Collins tried to get out of his embarrassment by saying that the British ought to take more care to prevent un-authorised persons getting their hands on lethal weapons, but he remained decidedly unhappy. This seizure had put the 'Irregulars', as they were now being called, into a relatively better position than the forces of the Provisional Government, who were com-

plaining of the niggardly supply of arms they were
receiving. With popular backing, Collins and the
Provisional Government, nevertheless, were taking a
stronger grip. Ruling as yet without electoral sanction, they were keeping the peace in a country
denuded of police, and Churchill once more spoke
optimistically. But he became depressed again when
he heard that several hundred Irregulars had taken
possession of Limerick. The threat of conflict there
was patched up, however, without the strong action
the British desired; and Churchill privately charged
the Provisional Government with being 'feeble,
apologetic, expostulatory' in comparison with their
enemies, who were seen to be 'active, audacious and
utterly shameless'. The 'feebleness' of the Provisional
Government was probably due partly to reluctance
to strike a first blow or make a provocative move in a
situation that Collins hoped to save by negotiation,
and partly to Mulcahy's insistence that the National
Army was not yet ready to face a major showdown
with the Irregulars.

2

A crisis situation was manifestly fast approaching. On
26 March the threatened Army Convention had been
held in spite of the prohibition of the Minister of
Defence, and the split, already in existence, was
confirmed by the appointment on 9 April of an
Executive and an Army Council with Liam Lynch
as Chief of Staff. There were now two armies in the
country — apart from the evacuating British army,
that is — one loyal to the Provisional Government,
and the other to the new Executive; and as restraint
between the two dissolved, the shooting began. By
6 May eight men had been killed and forty-nine
wounded in armed clashes. The Irregular Executive

grew increasingly bold, and Rory O'Connor, dis-
regarding Lynch, seized the Dublin Four Courts as
a headquarters, insisting at the same time that he and
some of his friends were no more prepared to stand
for de Valera and his external association scheme
than for the Treaty. Other buildings were occupied
simultaneously, and banks were raided for funds.
No action was taken by the Provisional Government
against O'Connor, but as a result of a peace conference arranged by the Archbishop of Dublin, a truce
was agreed which was intended to hold till the general
election.

Earlier the Irregulars had tried to break up public
meetings which were being held in support of the
Treaty. At one of these in Cork city, a gigantic affair
with three platforms for the speakers, shots were
fired causing a minor stampede. On that occasion
Collins dealt with the allegation that there had been
a surrender of the national position. Of that, he
declared, there was a single test: those who ended
in possession of the battlefield had won the war.
The British were leaving, and would be gone altogether
if de Valera and his friends would allow them to
depart.

On his way that night with Seán Mac Eoin to the
house of his sister, Mrs Powell, a man armed with a
pistol jumped out from behind the pier of a gate.
He shouted: 'Collins, I have you now,' but before
he could fire, Mac Eoin wrenched the gun from him,
saying to Collins: 'Will I shoot him?' 'No,' said
Collins. 'Let the bastard go.' This was not an isolated
experience. In April Collins disarmed and arrested
one of a group who attacked him and some of his
companions in Dublin, near Vaughan's Hotel. The
attackers did not apparently realise that Collins was
in the party. They were dealing, they thought, merely
with ordinary soldiers of the Provisional Government,

and there had been some loose talk about the likelihood that Irish blood would have to be spilt in order to achieve the freedom of the country. At the Archbishop's conference feelings ran high, particularly when Brugha referred to Griffith and Collins as agents of the British. Collins, irritated, leaned across the table towards Brugha and said: 'I suppose we are two of the ministers whose blood is to be waded through?' Brugha replied, quietly but distinctly: 'Yes, you are two.'[3]

3

Churchill, like everybody else, saw the occupation of the Four Courts as a major act of defiance of the Provisional Government and wanted Cope, his intermediary in Dublin, to find out immediately what the Irish government intended to do. Should not they ring round the mutineers, as he called them, and starve them out? Churchill was concerned, too, with the talks that Collins was conducting with de Valera about the forthcoming elections. He told Cope to do his utmost to dissuade him from a pitiful surrender to a man who did not even pretend to control his extremists. His anxiety was reduced somewhat when he noticed that the Free State troops were firing back when attacked and had turned the Irregulars out of Kilkenny Castle. He also admitted that there was a good deal to be said for the Provisional Government 'waiting its moment', putting up with the Four Courts situation until public opinion was exasperated.

By mid-May the Irish people had not yet had an opportunity of expressing an opinion on the Treaty; and the Collins—de Valera talks showing signs of breaking down, Collins sent Churchill word that the Provisional Government intended to fight, taking on the provincial areas first. He asked for ten thousand additional rifles, twenty thousand grenades, ten field guns and other military equipment. Churchill reacted negatively. Complaining to his colleagues of their treatment hitherto by the Provisional Government, he found difficulty in assenting to further large-scale issues of arms until he was satisfied that they would be used effectively against the Republican party. He considered that the sincerity of the Provisional Government should be put to the test; that they should be made to prove that they intended to deal resolutely with disorder in Dublin. He could not acquiesce in the Provisional Government sending expeditions into the country districts while continuing to parley with the rebels in Dublin; and he made it known that if they required a trench mortar to reduce the Four Courts, they could have one.

Nevertheless, on 20 May Collins and de Valera reached an agreement that on 16 June they would face the electorate together. The Treaty would be excluded as an issue; a coalition panel of candidates would be formed from both the pro- and anti-Treaty sections of Sinn Féin, the number allowed to each section being the same as its existing strength in the Dáil; and seats in a subsequent coalition government would be apportioned on the basis of the election results. Churchill was alarmed. This was an arrangement full of disaster. It would prevent an expression of opinion on the Treaty, and it would leave the Provisional Government in its existing helpless position. If, as was believed, de Valera was to be one of four Republican ministers in the coalition government, the Treaty would be definitely violated. At that stage some strong measures might become necessary such as the resumption of powers to occupy southern areas. From the wings Macready made rude noises intimating that he and his troops had eaten enough dirt; if an attack was made on them, he would teach Dublin a lesson with everything he had without bothering to wait for the government's decision or approval.

The reason given to Churchill by Collins for entering into this pact with de Valera was *force majeure*. There could be no real election, he said. Bands of armed men could seize and destroy ballot boxes. The state of disorder in the country would be aggravated, and England maddened with a series of outrages. There were fanatical Irregulars who were pure in motive though violent in method; behind them had gathered all the desperate elements of the population who pursued rapine for private gain. But it was impossible to draw distinctions between types of extremists: over all of them was the glamour of the Republic. He did not add that he was unwilling to use force against his own countrymen if it could at all be avoided. That was his basic position. He was prepared to make advances over and over again to those who opposed him, standing only on his fundamental obligation to maintain the freedom that had been won.

In so deferring action he exasperated his colleagues. Kevin O'Higgins, impatient at the delay, broke out occasionally, urging Collins to grasp the nettle and bring his growing forces to grips with the Irregulars. 'By God, we will!' Collins would say, thumping the table; but always he postponed the issue and tried to compromise. 'If we don't take action,' said Griffith, 'we will be considered the greatest poltroons in history.'[4] Griffith was thoroughly unhappy over the election pact and had done his utmost to prevent it. When asked at the cabinet meeting at which it was approved whether he favoured accepting it, he spent three whole minutes reflecting, pulling nervously at his tie and wiping his glasses. The other ministers waited in silence for his answer for what seemed a long time, and when he did assent he no longer addressed Collins as 'Mick' but with a noticeably formal 'Mr Collins'.[5]

Churchill was aware that a 'very democratic' constitution was being drafted in Dublin, and warned Collins not to take a final decision on it, much less to publish it, until the British government had seen it. When they did see it they immediately realised that it was a clear breach of the Treaty, the distance between the two documents being almost as great as when the Prime Minister had first begun his negotiations with de Valera twelve months earlier. This was deliberate on Collins's part: his aim and hope was to win over the anti-Treatyites with a document that, in Tom Jones's phrase, 'knocked the Treaty endways'. A formula, submitted for Collins by Hugh Kennedy, the Irish legal adviser, regarding the use of the name of the Crown, convinced the British that, if persisted in, a break was inevitable: they would be back to the pre-Treaty position. Jones conveyed this judgment to the Irish leaders separately. In response, Griffith said very little, and Jones suspected that he had not seen the formula before. Collins, intent on forcing the constitution through, reacted most pugnaciously. An unbridgeable gulf had been reached, he said, and he denounced the British ministers for being much more hostile than they had been during the Treaty negotiations. 'He talked on at a great rate in a picturesque way of going back to renew the struggle with his comrades Mulcahy and Mac Eoin, that the British seemed bent on war.' Jones was taken aback by this outburst, but Duggan, when he spoke to him, did not appear alarmed. The British ought to remember the life Collins had led during the previous three years, he said. Collins was very highly strung and overwrought and sometimes left their own meetings in a rage. There was no pretence on Duggan's part.

In letters to his fiancée Collins at this time complained that things were bad beyond words. It was really awful, he said, what he had to endure from the British owing to things that were being done by his opponents at home. He was almost without hope and wished to God that someone else would take over his job!

Lloyd George surprised his cabinet by displaying some sympathy with Collins's point of view. In the matter of such things as the summoning of parliament or the appointing of judges, the Irish were fed up with the Crown this and the Crown that, and no wonder, he said. However, after a lengthy discussion, during which Jones advised the Prime Minister to play for the isolation of Collins from his less extreme colleagues, a letter was sent to Griffith posing a series of questions to clear the air; and this was followed by a conference at which Griffith and Collins, having acknowledged that under the Treaty the Irish Free State would be inside the British Commonwealth, were told by Lloyd George that the question at issue was one between Republican and monarchical institutions. In the British system acts of state had to appear to be done in the name of the Crown, the Crown being a mystic term that simply stood for the power of the people.[6] Collins, of course, had another mystic term, the Republic, to contend with; and his failure to reduce the Crown element in the draft Irish constitution depressed him greatly, bringing as it did the possibility of civil war in Ireland so much nearer.

With talk of the Treaty perishing and the Anglo-Irish war being resumed, the Ulster situation had become a serious complicating factor. There had been fighting along the border from Belleek to Pettigo between the newly established Ulster Special Constabulary and what was described as the Republican IRA. Both villages, one wholly, the other partly, in

Northern Ireland territory, and the area between them were occupied by Republicans. Collins, Griffith and Cosgrave assured the British that they were in no way responsible and most strongly repudiated what had occurred, but Collins may well have been speaking tongue in cheek. On instructions from the War Office, two companies of the Lincolnshire Regiment entered the area, surrounded Pettigo and killed or captured the defenders.

The Prime Minister was profoundly disgusted by these developments and was warned by his civil servants that Churchill, after being splendid in the early days after the Treaty, was now so disappointed that he wanted to pull the whole plant out of the ground. The government was being manoeuvred into the worst possible situation by opponents of the Treaty, English and Irish, who wanted a break on the Ulster issue. Lloyd George therefore wrote a strongly worded letter to Churchill telling him to be on his guard against precipitate and provocative action that would commit them to a fight in the swamps of Lough Erne where they would be overwhelmed. They had done everything that Ulster could possibly expect to ensure its security, providing 57,000 armed men (9,000 troops and 48,000 'Specials'): the politicians must remain impartial and avoid creating incidents.

Their Ulster case was not a good one, he insisted. Although the area was not one-sixth of that of the Free State and had only one-third of its population, in two years 400 Catholics had been killed and 1,200 wounded without a single person being brought to justice. Several Protestants had also been murdered, but the murders of Catholics went on at the rate of three or four to one before Catholic reprisals attained their current dimensions. There had been unfounded allegations of concentration of Free State troops; but, when the British threatened the Pettigo salient with two brigades of infantry and a battery of artillery, all they found were twenty-three Free State soldiers on Free State territory in Pettigo, of whom seven were killed and fifteen captured. If war came out of this, he said, would it not make the government look rather ridiculous? Now an equally formidable force was marching against a rotten barrack at Belleek garrisoned by a friendly blacksmith and a handful of his associates. Mac Eoin (the blacksmith in question) was a strong Treaty man and had publicly denounced de Valera and the election pact. If he should be killed, it would be a disaster to the cause of reconciliation with the Irish race.

Churchill reacted badly to this 'telling off' and considered resigning; but that possibility was 'superseded by events'. Belleek village and fort were occupied by strong forces, and on the same day 'a most conciliatory' Hugh Kennedy conceded on all the crucial constitutional points. This came as an enormous relief to the London cabinet, who were in great difficulties trying to reach a decision as to the precise form of action which should be taken against the Provisional Government if they persisted with a constitution that did not conform to the Treaty.

As regards the source of the trouble in the North, Lloyd George thought that Sir Henry Wilson was as likely to be behind it as de Valera was. Since leaving the army he had become the Unionist MP for North Down and had been appointed as official adviser to the Northern Minister of Home Affairs on the organisation and control of the Special Constublary. He had been particularly obnoxious about the Treaty, believed that the weak-kneed British cabinet was on the way to swallowing the Collins—de Valera pact and the Republic, and advocated instead the reimposition of the Act of Union. When, therefore, he was assassinated outside his London house on 22 June sympathy for him in British government circles was muted. The question that arose immediately was: who had inspired the two Irishmen who were guilty of, and executed for, what Griffith and Collins called 'this anarchic deed'?

It is not inconceivable that Collins was responsible for the assassination, seeing it as a blow worth striking in the campaign hitherto waged unsuccessfully across the border in defence of the people in the North who were suffering at the hands of Wilson's Specials. But of this no evidence has so far been produced, apart from the statement given to a newspaper in 1953 by Joe Dolan of Collins's old intelligence group. This, without adducing any proof, declared that Collins instructed Sam Maguire, O/C Britain during the Anglo-Irish War, to carry out the execution, that Maguire conveyed the order to Reggie Dunne, O/C London, and that Dunne, together with his right-hand man, Joe O'Sullivan, did the job themselves. If this is true — and we do not deny the possibility — it means that Collins was involved in 'this anarchic deed', as indeed he was involved, in collusion with both pro- and anti-Treaty sections of the IRA, in the whole cross-border campaign behind the backs of the Irish and British governments. But at least one of his cabinet colleagues, Ernest Blythe, believed that Collins had nothing whatever to do with the assassination and put the blame on elements among the anti-Treaty forces who were out to make trouble for Collins with the British. Blythe saw Griffith and Collins together in the cabinet room preparing the 'anarchic deed' statement, and their demeanour convinced him that the death of Wilson had taken them both by surprise and left them genuinely appalled.[7] Their statement, which was given to the press by Griffith, suggested that Wilson's death was either an act of private vengeance or a pseudo-political affair which would be condemned and deplored by the vast majority of Irishmen who opposed Wilson's policies.[8]

Although there is a direct clash of evidence regarding Collins's complicity in the assassination, Blythe's testimony does not conflict with that part of Dolan's statement that deals with his personal involvement in an effort to save the lives of Dunne and O'Sullivan (except that previous biographers of Collins say that Cullen was the person sent on this mission and do not mention Dolan; it is possible that both men were involved). Collins could well have wanted to rescue Dunne and O'Sullivan regardless of whether or not he had any prior responsibility for the act for which they had been found guilty. 'I was sent across to interview Sam Maguire re attempted rescue,' Dolan's story goes. 'I returned to Dublin and put in a very favourable report to Michael Collins as to carrying out the job. . . . The Civil War then broke out, all were engaged elsewhere, the London Volunteers were split, and the two men were dead.'[9] It was also found impossible to carry out an order from Collins that an important personage should be taken as a hostage against the safety of Dunne and O'Sullivan.[10]

4

The constitutional dispute over, the general election went ahead on 16 June, but with no appeal from Collins on behalf of the agreed panel candidates. It produced a Dáil with 93 pro-Treaty seats (pro-Treaty Sinn Féin 58, Labour 17, Farmers 7, Independents 7, Dublin University Unionists 4) and 35 anti-Treaty Sinn Féin seats. The pact had obviously been abandoned by Collins and with it the idea of a coalition.

A House of Commons debate on Ireland was due, and Churchill was instructed by his cabinet colleagues to say that the vote of confidence the Provisional Government had received entitled the British to insist that the ambiguous position in Ireland should come to an end. Till that was done the imperial government would proceed no further in the execution of the Treaty; and if it were not done, they would be compelled to resume full liberty of action in any direction that might seem proper. Churchill in his speech added a note on the Northern situation that has a very modern ring about it. The greedy and criminal design of breaking down the Northern government, either by disorder from within or by incursion from without, he said, had got to die in the hearts of those who nourished it. The Sinn Féin party had got to realise, once and for all, that they would never win Ulster except by her own free will, and that the more they kicked against the pricks the worse it would be for them. This gave Collins an opportunity to draw to Churchill's notice the intention of the Northern authorities 'to abolish the enlightened and eminently fair system of proportional representation for Local Government elections', the effect of which would be 'to wipe out completely all effective representation of Catholic and National interests'. The nationalist strongholds of Co. Fermanagh, Co. Tyrone and Derry city, as well as several urban and rural districts, would go and completely anti-Catholic juntas would reign in their place. Collins thought that Churchill would agree that nothing could be more detrimental to the cause of peace.

On 26 June, the day the British threatened to resume 'full liberty of action', the Four Courts situation took a grave turn. A member of the garrison raided a garage to secure transport for another expedition to the North. He was arrested and, in retaliation, Major-General J. J. ('Ginger') O'Connell, Deputy Chief of Staff of the National Army, was kidnapped. A joint meeting was then called of the Dáil and Provisional Government cabinets, both locked up in Government Buildings, and a decision was taken to meet this challenge to their authority.

Collins saw that the thing he most feared was now unavoidable. He had hoped that the anti-Treaty people would not force him to go further than he would wish to defend the Treaty. There were men among the Irregulars that he had been prepared to go almost any distance to satisfy, men he preferred to a dozen de Valeras, and the thought of turning the guns on them was abhorrent to him. But the hated thing had to be done, and done with Churchill's ugly speech ringing in his ears. 'Let Churchill come over and do his own dirty work,' he snapped. But the decision to act was not reversed. Instead an ultimatum was issued that night to the Four Courts garrison to vacate the buildings, and on their refusal to do so the National Army went into action. They invested the vast complex and attacked it with guns borrowed from the British, but so inexpertly that some of the shells fell in the grounds of the British army GHQ, causing Macready and his staff to wonder whether this had been done deliberately.

It was some days before the surrender came. Then Brugha was killed when the National Army turned its attention to a block of hotels in O'Connell Street. Collins was deeply moved when he heard what had occurred, and grieved even more when he was told that his dearest friend, Harry Boland, had been shot dead in the hotel in Skerries where he had been staying. He burst into tears, giving vent to an emotion Piaras Béaslaí had witnessed when Collins read a letter from a woman whose son, under sentence of death, had been saved by the Treaty. Collins had written an extraordinary letter to Boland a few days before: 'Harry, it has come to this!' it ran. 'Of all things it has come to this. It is in my power to arrest you and destroy you. This I cannot do.' And, in words he must have often used in the hope of causing former comrades to end their resistance, he ended: 'If you will think over the influence which has dominated you, it should change your ideas. You are walking under false colours. If no words of mine will change your attitude, then you are beyond all hope — my hope.'

On 30 June, the day the Four Courts surrendered, the Public Record Office, which was part of the complex, blew up by some terrible mischance, causing an appalling destruction of national archives. Churchill, to a stupid and tactless message of congratulation to the Provisional Government, added a *bon mot:* 'The archives of the Four Courts may be scattered,' he said, 'but the title-deeds of Ireland are safe.' A variant that he put into circulation later ran: 'Better a state without archives than archives without a state.' He recognised, however, that congratulations from London were liable to be misunderstood when he learned that the Provisional Government were being blamed for having gone into action at the behest of the British. He warned his colleagues to make it clear in their speeches that the Irish had acted on their own initiative.

The fighting in Dublin city ended on 5 July, leaving one half of O'Connell Street, as well as the Four Courts, in ruins. On 12 July a War Council was instituted by the Provisional Government with Collins as Commander-in-Chief, Mulcahy as Minister of Defence and Chief of Staff, and O'Duffy as Deputy Chief of Staff and GOC for the south-west. They donned army uniforms, and Collins and Mulcahy took up quarters in Portobello Barracks. Other men prominent in politics had similarly begun to reorganise their lives. De Valera, though snubbed originally by Rory O'Connor, rejoined his old Volunteer battalion as a private, declaring that those under attack from the Provisional Government were 'the best and bravest of our nation'. After the Dublin surrenders he made his way to Liam Lynch's headquarters at Clonmel and was appointed adjutant to the Republican Director of Operations, Seán Moylan. Childers also went south and, with the rank of staff captain and carrying a revolver that Collins had once given him and which was eventually to cost him his life, continued to issue a Republican publicity sheet.

Collins too began to move out to the country, intent on clearing up the military situation as speedily as possible. He had no intention of merely trying to direct operations from a Dublin office. A representative example can be given of how he operated: he was in Maryboro on 22 July, where, having consulted the local officers, he issued the following series of directions:

(1) Occupy *Tullamore* with fifty men on Sunday.
(2) Columns will move from *Maryboro* and *Birr* in the direction of *Kilcormac* to clear up the Irregulars there. When this is done a post with twenty-five men will be established in that place.
(3) *Nenagh* will clear the country to the South to *Birdhill* and *Limerick*.
(4) Reduce *Abbeyleix* to thirty [men], ditto *Durrow* to thirty [men].
(5) Occupy *Mountmellick*.
(6) When *Tullamore* occupied and some clearing up done in that area, a post will be established in *Philipstown*.
(7) *Maryboro* will operate with a column in area of *Clonaslee*.

The extent of the task confronting him can be very roughly gauged from the fact that at the beginning of August the Irregulars controlled in Munster alone large parts of the counties of Limerick, Waterford, Kerry and Tipperary, as well as the whole of Co. Cork, including Cork city. In the area from Galway to Donegal and from Westmeath to Westport in Co. Mayo, a vast tract of country over which Seán Mac Eoin had been appointed divisional commander, his opponents had three divisions on his west flank and a brigade on his east flank, in addition to a division that was within striking distance of his Athlone head-quarters.[11] But in all of these areas there were some pro-Treaty Volunteers.

Collins, aided by Mulcahy, prepared a general strategy and discussed its detailed implementation with the GOCs. In Athlone, for example, which they visited, they arranged that Mac Eoin would undertake a simultaneous operation on both flanks involving a landing from the sea at Westport. This had a demoralising effect on the enemy force despite their superiority in numbers and equipment, except that Mac Eoin had an armoured car[12] and later acquired a field gun. The programme for the clearance of Munster proceeded on similar lines. A landing at Fenit enabled Tralee to be taken without serious resistance and forced Co. Limerick open. Cork city, the second largest con-urbation in the Free State area, then remained to be taken along with an area to the east and west of it. A tough fight was anticipated, but when Emmet Dalton was put ashore at Passage West with some five hundred men on 10 August he was able to take the city with little difficulty and to move as far west as Macroom. Simultaneous landings had taken place at Youghal and Union Hall. There followed from these manoeuvres an almost complete collapse of the anti-Treaty forces in the south of the country. Fermoy, the last town held by them, fell on 11 August, com-pelling Lynch to retreat with his staff into the hills.

Thereafter the fight continued on old familiar lines — bridges were blown up, roads trenched, and ambushes prepared — but this time the enemy was Collins and his men.

5

On about 9 August, as the military operation in Munster was reaching its climax, Collins began a tour of inspection of the places recovered by the National Army. He was in Tralee on the 12th when he received a message that Griffith had died suddenly. He can hardly have been surprised by the news. Since the previous autumn he had known of Griffith's ill-health, and he had had a stern reminder of it when obliged one night practically to carry the President, whose appearance was horrifying, down the stairs of Government Buildings.[13] Utterly exhausted, Griffith had agreed to enter a nursing home on the other side of Merrion Street, but the doctors could not get him to rest properly. He was up and about his room working at his papers and crossing over to his office nearly every day. He died bending down to tie a boot-lace. The strain of the Civil War, on top of everything else he had been through, including his disagreements with Collins, may have been his final undoing. His doctor friend Oliver St John Gogarty was sure it was and, quoting Tennyson, said that Griffith had perished by the people he had made. Obviously expecting the worst, he had left a letter calling on these people to stand firm for the Free State: it was their national need and economic salvation. A man who knew Griffith well, P. S. O'Hegarty, saw him in his room on the second day of the Four Courts fighting and was shocked at the change in him. He was obviously sick unto death, sick in his soul. He sat there brooding, now and again writing, with all his gaiety and humour gone from him, like a man waiting for some inevitable thing. 'Of course,' he said, 'those fellows will assassinate myself and Collins.'[14] At his graveside Collins was standing alone when Dr Fogarty, the Bishop of Killaloe, spoke to him. 'Michael,' he said, 'you should be prepared — you may be the next.' Collins turned. 'I know,' he said simply.

He had returned to Dublin immediately he heard of Griffith's death, but resumed his southern tour when the funeral was over. He was advised not to do so by some of his colleagues, one of whom said that a Commander-in-Chief should take no such risks. He insisted on going, however. He wanted particularly to see for himself how things were in Cork, and he still had hopes of personally inducing influential anti-Treatyites to call off the fighting. He threatened that if he could not go by car, he would go on his old bicycle! 'No one's going to shoot me in my own county,' he added. Suffering from a cold and appearing somewhat depressed, he left the city about six o'clock on the morning of 20 August with an armoured car escort and, making some stops on the way, was in Limerick shortly after midday. He visited Maryboro jail to discuss with an anti-Treaty prisoner the continuing problem of reaching a peaceful and speedy end to the fighting between old comrades. The prisoner, Thomas Malone, was a man he admired, and having talked to him, he left the jail feeling that 'the three Toms' — Tom Malone, Tom Barry and Tom Hales (the latter two being prominent anti-Treaty commandants) — if they came together in an IRB setting, might succeed where negotiations with men like Liam Lynch had failed. Travelling via Mallow he reached Cork about half-past eight, and that evening and all the next day, in the company of Emmet Dalton and his staff, he discussed the problems of the area, military and civil, including the steps being taken to counter the manipulation of public revenues and bank moneys by the Irregulars. He inspected military posts, interviewed many people, motored as far as Macroom, and visited relatives and friends. He wrote to Cosgrave: 'It would be a big thing to get Civic Guards both here and in Limerick. Civil administration urgent everywhere in the South. The people are splendid.'

Starting after six o'clock on the morning of 22 August, he was on the road again in convoy and hoped to cover the country to as far west as Bantry. He got no further, however, than Clonakilty, where his entrance to the town was delayed by having to help to remove felled trees that blocked the road. Clonakilty was, of course, the heart of Collins's homeland, and people flocked from all directions to greet him. His brother Johnnie came in from the fields, and with him and other members of the family and some neighbours Mick drank a pint of the Wrastler in the local pub, the Five Alls. He drove to Roscarbery and Skibbereen after lunch, and then to Bandon: everywhere it was the same: warm welcoming crowds and much business to be hurriedly done.

The light was fading when the convoy finally began the roundabout return journey to Cork. A motor-cyclist scout and a Crossley tender carrying ten men under Seán O'Connell preceded the touring-car, in which Collins and Dalton sat behind the drivers, with an armoured car, the *Slievenamon,* bringing up the rear. They travelled the same road as on the way down, following the directions given to them by a man they had stopped to consult. This man, however, happened to be an Irregular, and he immediately reported the convoy, adding the important detail that Collins was the central figure in it. On the reasonable assumption that the blocked roads would force the convoy to return by the same route, it was decided to lay an ambush. A dray was dragged out into the middle of the road at a chosen spot in the valley of Béal na mBláth and its wheels removed, and the ambushing party lay around all day waiting for an eventuality which they almost despaired of when, at about half-past seven, the convoy was seen approaching. What then happened is related by Emmet Dalton, whom we paraphrase:

We had just turned a corner when a sudden and heavy fusilade of machine-gun fire swept the road in front of us and behind us, shattering the windscreen of our car. I shouted to the driver — 'Drive like hell!', but Collins, placing his hand on the man's shoulder, said — 'Stop! Jump out and we'll fight them.' We leaped from the car and took what cover we could. The armoured car backed up the road and opened heavy fire on the attackers, but the machine-gun jammed after a short time. The occupants of the tender cleared the old dray out of the way. Collins and I, with Joe Dolan who was near us, opened a rapid rifle fire on our seldom visible enemies, and we continued to fire for about twenty minutes without casualties when a lull in the attack became noticeable. Collins jumped to his feet and walked over behind the armoured car, obviously to obtain a better view of the enemy's position. He remained there, firing occasional shots. Suddenly I heard him shout — 'Come on, boys!' There they are, running up the road.' I immediately opened fire upon two figures that were in view. When I next turned around Collins had left the car position and had run about fifteen yards back up the road. Here he dropped into the prone firing position and opened up. Presently his firing ceased, and I fancied I heard a faint cry of 'Emmet!' O'Connell and I rushed to the spot with a dreadful fear clutching our hearts.

We found our beloved Chief and friend lying motionless, firmly gripping his rifle, across which his head was resting. There was a fearful gaping wound at the base of the skull and behind the right ear. He could not speak. O'Connell whispered the Act of Contrition and was rewarded by a slight pressure of the hand. I kept up a burst of rapid fire, whilst O'Connell dragged Collins into cover behind the armoured car. By this time he was certainly dead. As the attack abated, we took the body into the touring-car, and with his head resting on my shoulder, our awe-stricken party continued the journey.

From the ambush point at Béal na mBláth the dispirited convoy went to Crookstown where a priest performed the solemn last rites in the light of head-lamps. Moving on, the convoy took a road which, if it had been followed, would have plunged the cars over a broken bridge onto the Cork—Macroom railway line forty feet below. They had to reverse, and on a 'carpet' of army greatcoats, blankets and petrol tins crossed four fields to the main Cork road. Even then the armoured car had to be abandoned temporarily and the body of Collins shouldered for some of the way. It was three o'clock next morning before the city was reached. 'So long as I live', said Dalton, 'the memory of that nightmare ride will haunt me.' From Cork the remains were brought by boat to Dublin and buried in Glasnevin.

The grief of the nation was unmistakable. 'I'm really too sad and too sick to write,' an IRB man said. 'If all belonging to me were dead I'd not feel half so bad.'[15] That was the universal reaction. It reached into the prisons and internment camps. Tom Barry saw about a thousand of Collins's prisoners on their knees, praying for a man who in his brief life had enriched and exalted Ireland and in dying had reduced and impoverished mankind.[16]

* * *

The tragedy of his death went far beyond the manner of it or the place where it occurred, and far beyond the killing in combat of a young Irishman of notable appearance and physique. Many such men unfortunately died in that way and were speedily forgotten. Collins's case was vastly different. He was anything but a typical young Irish soldier, though he would have been happy to regard himself as such. He was a guerrilla genius, and much more besides. At the age of thirty-one, and in a 'public life' of barely five years, he was already a national and international figure. Greatness had touched him, leaving him on the threshold of a career that could well have brought him to heights to which no Irishman before him had attained. It was in such terms that the common people of Ireland thought of him, expecting that his gallantry, his leadership and the gifts of organisation and statesmanship he was displaying would surely be at their service for many years to come. Béal na mBláth brutally ended that expectation, leaving it to others to secure what he had in mind when, looking to his country's political destiny, he had spoken of stepping-stones, of the Treaty he had so greatly helped to engineer containing within itself the freedom to achieve the ultimate freedom to which all nations aspire. That freedom was achieved, in so far as it could be achieved. A quarter-century of uneasy dominionship was succeeded by a republic as free as any in the world, a republic accepted by Irishmen whether they originally followed Collins's lead or not. That is all to the good, and yet it is now apparent

[146] that the most tragic element in Collins's death was that it occurred at all, for it was as unnecessary as the bitter and ruinous civil war which the compassionate realist strove so hard and risked so much to avoid.

References

Chapter 1: The Road to Insurrection (pp. 1–25)

1. O'Hegarty, *Victory of Sinn Féin*, 23–4.
2. Ryan, *Remembering Sion*, 235.
3. NLI, MS. 13329 (3).
4. Thornton Memoir.
5. Ensor, *England, 1870–1914*, 418–19.
6. Ó Broin, *Revolutionary Underground*, 143.
7. Gwynn, *Life of John Redmond*, 145.
8. John (Jock) McGallogly in conversation with the author.
9. O'Connor, *The Big Fellow*, 37.
10. FitzGerald, *Memoirs*, 144.
11. Tobin Papers; Béaslaí, *Michael Collins*, I, 367.
12. O'Brien, *Forth the Banners Go*, 136.
13. *Ibid.*, 136–7.
14. Ryan, 215.
15. Sweeney in Martin, ed., *The Easter Rising, 1916, and University College, Dublin.*

Chapter 2: The Organiser of Resistance (pp. 25–42)

1. Scott, *Political Diaries*, 205.
2. Lyons, *Ireland since the Famine*, 381.
3. Pakenham, *Peace by Ordeal*, 30.
4. O'Brien, 144.
5. Brennan, *Allegiance*, 154.
6. Ó Muirthile Memoir.
7. Lyons, 397.
8. O'Malley, *On Another Man's Wound*, 76–7.
9. O'Hegarty, *Victory of Sinn Féin*, 75.

Chapter 3: Director of Intelligence (pp. 43–69)

1. Kavanagh in *Capuchin Annual* (1969), 354.
2. O'Donoghue, *No Other Law*, 120.
3. Thornton Memoir.
4. Dalton, *With the Dublin Brigade*, 84.

[148]

5. Mulcahy, 'Note on the Differences between Cathal Brugha and Stack and Other Members of the Volunteer Executive and Cabinet' (Mulcahy Papers, P7/D/96).
6. Risteárd Mulcahy in *An Cosantóir* (forthcoming, 1980).
7. Stapleton in *Capuchin Annual* (1969), 370.
8. O'Daly Memoir.
9. Stapleton in *Capuchin Annual* (1969), 369.
10. Tobin in conversation with Geoffrey Hand, 24 Sep. 1961.
11. *Irish Independent*, Michael Collins Memorial Foundation Supplement, 20 Aug. 1966.
12. O'Hegarty, *Victory of Sinn Féin*, 138.
13. Thornton Memoir.
14. Gilbert, *Winston S. Churchill*, IV, Pt 2, 1090.
15. *Ibid.*, 1142.
16. Gaughan, *Memoirs of Constable Jeremiah Mee*, 130–50.
17. Townshend in *English Historical Review* XCIV, No. 371 (Apr. 1979), 327.
18. Sturgis Diary.
19. Gaughan, 189–90.
20. Townshend, *British Campaign*, 223.
21. Brennan Memoir.

Chapter 4: The Pursuit of Peace (pp. 69–85)

1. Townshend, *British Campaign*, 152.
2. *Ibid.*, 155.
3. *Ibid.*, 152.
4. Barry, *Guerilla Days*, 164–6.
5. Sturgis Diary.
6. Townshend, *British Campaign*, 174.
7. Townshend in *English Historical Review* XCIV, No. 371 (Apr. 1979), 326.
8. Mulcahy, 'Note on the Differences'.
9. Tobin in conversation with Geoffrey Hand, 24 Sep. 1961.
10. *Ibid.*
11. Townshend in *English Historical Review* XCIV, No. 371 (Apr. 1979), 338 (quoting Mulcahy Papers).
12. Béaslaí, II, 218.
13. Risteárd Mulcahy in *Studies* LXVII, No. 267 (autumn 1978), 195; and in *An Cosantóir* (forthcoming, 1980).
14. Townshend, *British Campaign*, 179–80.
15. Townshend in *English Historical Review* XCIV, No. 371 (Apr. 1979), 342.
16. Thornton Memoir.
17. Townshend, *British Campaign*, 80.

18. Darling, *So It Looks to Me*, 210–13.
19. Townshend in *English Historical Review* XCIV, No. 371 [149] (Apr. 1979), 326, 340.
20. Brennan Memoir.
21. Dalton, 62.
22. Thornton Memoir.
23. Taylor, *Michael Collins*, 110.

Chapter 5: Negotiating with the Enemy (pp. 86–119)

1. MacLysaght, *Changing Times*, 130.
2. O'Hegarty, *History of Ireland under the Union*, 772.
3. Béaslaí, II, 275.
4. *Ibid.*, 276.
5. Taylor, 170–1.
6. Longford and O'Neill, *Eamon de Valera*, 148.
7. Cronin, *McGarrity Papers*, 109–11.
8. *Ibid.*, 125.
9. Taylor, 165.
10. Mulcahy, 'Note on the Differences'.
11. *Ibid.*
12. *Ibid.*
13. Lyons, 431.
14. Sturgis Diary.
15. Pakenham, 106.
16. O'Malley, *Singing Flame*, 33.
17. Béaslaí, II, 270–1.
18. White, *Kevin O'Higgins*, 15–16.
19. Ó Broin, 196.
20. Birkenhead, *F. E. Smith, First Earl of Birkenhead*, 382–3.
21. Ó Broin, 181–3; see also p. 40 above.
22. Risteárd Mulcahy in *Studies* LXVII, No. 267 (autumn 1978), 190.
23. Davis, *Arthur Griffith and Non-Violent Sinn Féin*, 163.
24. Mulcahy, 'Note on the Differences'.
25. *Ibid.*
26. *Ibid.*
27. Taylor, 179.
28. *Ibid.*, 163.
29. Jones, *Whitehall Diary*, III, 179.
30. *Ibid.*, 180.
31. Sturgis Diary.
32. Jones, 180.
33. *Ibid.*, 182.
34. *Ibid.*, 183.

35. Ó Broin, 196.
36. Kathleen MacKenna to author, 16 Oct. 1978.
37. R. H. S. Crossman in *The Guardian*, 4 Dec. 1959.
38. Jones, 183.
39. Kathleen MacKenna to author, 16 Oct. 1978.
40. Pakenham, 257.
41. Risteárd Mulcahy in *An Cosantóir* (forthcoming, 1980).
42. Healy, *Letters and Leaders of My Day*, II, 651.
43. White, 69.
44. *Ibid.*, 77.
45. Ó Broin, 206, 224.

Chapter 6: Death in the Fading Light (pp. 119—46)
1. Kevin R. O'Shiel, who was with Collins that day, in conversation with the author.
2. Buckland, *Irish Unionism* 2, 157.
3. O'Brien, 220.
4. White, 90.
5. Ó Lúing, *Art Ó Gríofa*, 396.
6. Jones, 202—8.
7. Blythe in conversation with the author.
8. *Irish Independent*, 22 Jun. 1922.
9. Dolan in *Sunday Press*, 27 Sep. 1953.
10. Seán Ó Lúing in *Irish Times*, 20 May 1961.
11. Mac Eoin's unpublished autobiography.
12. *Ibid.*
13. Ó Broin in *Studies* LXV, No. 261 (spring 1977), 33.
14. O'Hegarty, *Victory of Sinn Féin*, 122—3.
15. Patrick McCartan to Joe McGarrity, quoted in Cronin, 123.
16. Barry, 180; Pakenham, 270.

Bibliography

Unpublished sources
Bureau of Military History Chronology, Parts I—III
Brennan Memoir (in the possession of General Michael Brennan)
Collins Papers (NLI)
Seán Mac Eoin's unpublished autobiography (in the custody of Mrs Alice Mac Eoin)
Richard Mulcahy, 'Note on the Differences between Cathal Brugha and Stack and Other Members of the Volunteer Executive and Cabinet' (Mulcahy Papers, P7/D/96, Department of Archives, UCD)
O'Daly Memoir (NLI microfilm p4548)
Ó Muirthile Memoir (Mulcahy Papers, P7/52, Department of Archives, UCD)
Sturgis Diary (PRO, London, 30/59, 1—5)
Thornton Memoir (in the possession of the Thornton family)
Tobin Papers (in the possession of the Tobin family)

Published sources
Barry, Tom, *Guerilla Days in Ireland*, Dublin 1949; repr. Tralee 1962
Béaslaí, Piaras, *Michael Collins and the Making of a New Ireland*, 2 vols, Dublin 1926
Birkenhead, Frederick, 2nd Earl of, *F. E. Smith, First Earl of Birkenhead*, London 1959
Brennan, Robert, *Allegiance*, Dublin 1950
Buckland, Patrick, *Irish Unionism 2: Ulster Unionism and the Origins of Northern Ireland, 1886—1922*, Dublin 1973
Cronin, Seán, *The McGarrity Papers*, Tralee 1972
Dáil Éireann, *Minutes of Proceedings of the First Parliament of the Republic of Ireland, 1919—1921. Official Record*, Dublin [1921]
Dáil Éireann, *Private Sessions of Second Dáil*, Dublin 1972
Dáil Éireann, *Official Report, Debate on the Treaty between Great Britain and Ireland signed in London on the 6th December 1921*, Dublin [1922]

[152] Dalton, Charles, *With the Dublin Brigade, 1917–1921*, London 1929

Darling, William, *So It Looks to Me*, London 1952

Davis, Richard, *Arthur Griffith and Non-Violent Sinn Féin*, Tralee 1974

Ensor, R. C. K., *England, 1870–1914*, Oxford 1936

FitzGerald, Desmond, *Memoirs*, London 1969

Fitzpatrick, David, *Politics and Irish Life, 1913–1921: Provincial Experience of War and Revolution*, Dublin 1977

Forester, Margery, *Michael Collins, the Lost Leader*, London 1971

Gaughan, J. Anthony, *Austin Stack*, Tralee 1977

Gaughan, J. Anthony, *Memoirs of Constable Jeremiah Mee, RIC*, Tralee 1975

Gilbert, Martin, *Winston S. Churchill*, Vol. IV (and Companion Volumes I–III), London 1977

Gwynn, Denis R., *The Life of John Redmond*, London 1932

Harkness, D. W., 'Britain and the Independence of the Dominions' in T. W. Moody, ed., *Nationality and the Pursuit of National Independence*, Belfast 1978

Harkness, D. W., *The Restless Dominion*, London 1969

Healy, T. M., *Letters and Leaders of My Day*, 2 vols, London 1928

Irish Independent, Michael Collins Memorial Foundation Supplement, 20 Aug. 1966

Jones, Thomas, *Whitehall Diary*, Vol. III: *Ireland, 1918–25*, ed. Keith Middlemas, London 1971

Kavanagh, Seán, 'The Irish Volunteers' Intelligence Organisation', *Capuchin Annual* (1969)

Longford, Earl of (Frank Pakenham) and T. P. O'Neill, *Eamon de Valera*, London 1970

Lyons, F. S. L., *Ireland since the Famine*, London 1971; revised ed., London 1973

Macardle, Dorothy, *The Irish Republic*, London 1937; revised ed., London 1968

MacLysaght, Edward, *Changing Times*, Gerrard's Cross 1978

Mulcahy, Risteárd, 'The Development of the Irish Volunteers, 1916–1922' (address to the Irish Military History Society, 9 Nov. 1978), *An Cosantóir* (forthcoming, 1980)

Mulcahy, Risteárd, 'Michael Collins and the Making of a New Ireland', *Studies* LXVII, No. 267 (autumn 1978)

Óglach, An t- (1918–22)

O'Brien, William, *Forth the Banners Go*, ed. Edward MacLysaght, Dublin 1969

Ó Broin, Leon, *Dublin Castle and the 1916 Rising: The Story of Sir Matthew Nathan*, Dublin 1966; revised ed., London 1970 [153]

Ó Broin, Leon, 'Joseph Brennan, Civil Servant Extraordinary', *Studies* LXV, No. 261 (spring 1977)

Ó Broin, Leon, 'Revolutionary Nationalism in Ireland' in T. W. Moody, ed., *Nationality and the Pursuit of National Independence*, Belfast 1978

Ó Broin, Leon, *Revolutionary Underground: The Story of the Irish Republican Brotherhood, 1858–1924*, Dublin 1976

O'Connor, Frank, *The Big Fellow*, revised ed., Dublin 1965

O'Donoghue, Florence, *No Other Law*, London 1954

O'Hegarty, P. S., *A History of Ireland under the Union, 1801–1922*, London 1952

O'Hegarty, P. S., *The Victory of Sinn Féin*, Dublin 1924

Ó Lúing, Seán, *Art Ó Gríofa*, Dublin 1953

O'Malley, Ernie, *On Another Man's Wound*, London 1936; repr. as *Army without Banners*, London 1967

O'Malley, Ernie, *The Singing Flame*, Dublin 1978

Pakenham, Frank (Earl of Longford), *Peace by Ordeal*, London 1935; repr. London 1972

Ryan, Desmond, *Remembering Sion*, London 1934

Scott, C. P., *Political Diaries*, London 1970

Stapleton, William J., 'Michael Collins's Squad', *Capuchin Annual* (1969)

Sweney, J. A., 'In the GPO: The Fighting Men' in F. X. Martin, ed., *The Easter Rising, 1916, and University College, Dublin*, Dublin 1966

Taylor, Rex, *Michael Collins*, London 1958; repr. London 1961

Townshend, Charles, *The British Campaign in Ireland, 1919–1921*, Oxford 1975

Townshend, Charles, 'The Irish Republican Army and the Development of Guerrilla Warfare, 1916–1921', *English Historical Review* XCIV, No. 371 (Apr. 1979)

White, Terence de Vere, *Kevin O'Higgins*, London 1948

Index